with thanks and
warm regards

But We Are Different...

A Thought for Browsers

What 99.9 per cent quality would mean for the USA:

- One hour of unsafe drinking water per day

- Two unsafe landings at O'Hare Airport, Chicago, each day

- 16,000 lost pieces of mail each hour

- 22,000 incorrect prescriptions each year

- 500 incorrect surgical operations performed each week

- 19,000 newborn babies dropped at birth by doctors each year

- 22,000 cheques deducted from the wrong account each hour

- Your heart fails to beat 32,000 times each year

Statistics from Baptist Memorial Hospital of Memphis, Tennessee.

But We Are Different...

QUALITY FOR THE SERVICE SECTOR

John Macdonald

This book is dedicated
to the legion of thinking
women who contribute
to the quality revolution

First published in 1994 by Management Books 2000 Ltd
125A The Broadway, Didcot, Oxfordshire OX11 8AW

Printed and bound in Great Britain by BPC   Wheatons Ltd, Exeter

British Library Cataloguing in Publication Data is available

ISBN 1-85251-131-1 (Hardcover)
1-85252-123-6 (Paperback)

PREFACE

This book is about the management of services in the new world in which the customer is king. It's about releasing the untapped potential of people within service organisations. It's about a vision: the journey to total and continuous improvement. It's designed to help those executives, managers and administrators who are interested in the quality revolution and want to begin the journey.

The book describes the tools of quality management and the practical management steps required to change the culture of organisations. However, it is not intended to be a tool-bound textbook. It has been written in everyday language to appeal to the minds and hearts of those responsible for driving change.

But We Are Different... can be viewed as a companion volume to *Global Quality – the New Management Culture* written in collaboration with John Piggott. That book had a tendency to draw its examples from the manufacturing industries. Many managers in the service industries and the public sector really believe that they are different so that the lessons of manufacturing do not apply to them. This book demonstrates that they are both right and wrong.

John Macdonald
Autumn 1993

ACKNOWLEDGEMENTS

For this author, writing has to be a gregarious exercise. Ideas, thoughts or concepts do not flow unaided or come as blinding flashes of inspiration. Somehow they have to be stimulated and worried into a cohesive whole with the help of others. Therefore these acknowledgments are a recognition of my debt to a host of stimulating and thinking friends. In a sense they are co-authors.

This book has a substantial base of practical experience in implementing quality initiatives. A major contribution therefore comes from working with colleagues over the years. From Honeywell Information Systems (now Bull) my thanks are due to Brian Long, Rene Berger, Gerry Cregan, Frank Dewar, Tom Frame, Arnie Johnson and many others. A major contribution comes from colleagues at the REL Consultancy Group in the UK and in the USA.

Clients are an inspiration to any consultant. When is all said and done they support the process of putting theory into practice with real money. I have and continue to enjoy the partnership and owe them a debt far beyond mere fees. Over a decade many have become close friends and several have contributed to this book. For obvious reasons it would be invidious to recognise all of them under this heading but some are acknowledged individually for their special help. For keeping the wolf from the door and for giving me time to share thoughts I can only hope that this band of friends continues to grow.

A substantial proportion of friends and fellow practitioners who shared their experience and thoughts are women – a fact which inspired the dedication. Perhaps women have a special talent which is suited to the new management philosophy. From my own country my thanks are due to Pat Freeman-Cramp of the National Health Service, Cheryl Horwitz, Jenny Riley, Wendy Walden and above all to Sarah Dawson, not only as a valued friend and colleague but also as a major contributor to the development of concepts. Abroad my appreciation is extended to Linda Rae Baldwin and Linda Vincze of Florida, to Catherine Popowitz of Cross Cultural Communications,

Chicago, to Dr Faith Ralston of Faith Ralston and Company of Minneapolis (a major contributor), to Susan Graves of Philadelphia (an author in her own right), to the incomparable Pat Tyre of Connecticut, to Michelle de Valbois of Paris, and special thanks are due to Joan Stroble of Kingston, NY, who broke a writer's block at a vital moment – and finally, for her unceasing support, to Sheila Stevenson of Chicago.

Returning to males, thanks are due to those who have contributed by providing ideas or by reading the manuscript. These include old colleagues Jim Bull and John Piggott, Bob Collins, Vice President of Quality, American National Can, George and Helen Farmer of Grimaud, France, Harry Gibson, Mike Hansen of Society Bank, Ohio, Steven Hunt of Arthur Andersen, Chicago, Wayne Kost of Florida, Joe McNally, CEO of Compaq Computer UK, J.K. Chandna of Qualteam Consultants, New Delhi, India, Bob Parent of Washington, DC, and Dr Stephen Tanner of the Prudential Assurance Company.

I should also recognise that authors are difficult to live with or be around, or at least this one is. So special mention to my amazing children Stephen, Sarah (who word-processes all my illegible writing) and Nicholas, each of whom, in partnership with Sharon, Stephen and Liz are successful in their own right and are a tribute to my wife Anne. Under this heading are also included Robert Postema of Management Books 2000 and my patient literary agent, Mike Sharland.

As in my last book, my final acknowledgement is to the Eagles, or, to the uninitiated, Crystal Palace Football Club, who inspire all manner of moods and passions.

CONTENTS

1. INTRODUCTION AND OVERVIEW

There is a commonly held belief that service organisations lag far behind the manufacturing industries in the application of total quality management principles. There is some truth in this perception. Yet one service company in Britain was building a massive business totally based on all these concepts long before Philip Crosby published his book *Quality is Free*.

Marks and Spencer were the principal advisers in the scripting of a film entitled 'Right First Time', produced by the British Productivity Association back in the sixties. Though using slightly different words, the film demonstrated the application of Crosby's Four Absolutes. But much, much further the company was also applying Deming's Fourteen Points for management in its structured relationship with its customers, suppliers and employees. Marks and Spencer now own Brook's Brothers, the epitome of clothing quality for many American executives and managers. If only we had fully understood and followed the concepts M & S were demonstrating in the fifties and sixties Britain would have rivalled Japan as the quality centre of the world. But it was not to be.

In retrospect, the service organisations have followed the same path as the manufacturing industries. Product quality or the basic service quality was always important but it was measured in levels of customer satisfaction in which ninety something per cent was satisfactory. Improved quality was also associated with inspection or checking, which was by definition expensive. Quality was therefore a compromise between what could be justified competitively and cost.

The service organisations also exhibited the same lack of comprehension about who was really responsible for quality. Most quality initiatives were based on training the lowest level of the organisation in customer care and courtesy. Management had little or no contact with the daily customer and neither talked nor listened to those who did. Many service companies saw quality as a courteous pretty girl out front and never mind the chaos in the back office. As long as this was the norm it was sufficient to maintain a reasonably profitable business.

Then came a new competitive force. The new force was an aroused and less easily satisfied customer. The consumers of services had been taught that they did not automatically have to accept what the service organisation deemed they would accept. The Japanese may have started the revolution in perception but the consumer associations and the legislator, conscious of their votes, have supported these aspirations.

Again, this experience differs little from that of the manufacturing industries though it took a little longer to make itself felt. But manufacturing has responded and now the searchlight is solidly centred on the service organisations: the word 'organisation' is used to some purpose. The service *industries* might have been expected to face similar pressures to that faced by manufacturing industries but the consumer revolution or market-driven economy has wider impact. The entrenched power of tradition and money is also under attack. Surgeons, doctors, barristers, solicitors, professors and teachers are, to their horror, being questioned as to the real quality of service they are providing to the consumer. Each in their own way are mobilising the power of their professional associations or unions to hold the pass and cushion the shock. But the power amassed against them appears to be inexorable and sooner or later they will be forced to respond. If they do, the word 'professional' may once again attain the same level of respect it once commanded. So this book intends to venture far beyond the basic service industries in examining quality and the consumer. At its broadest it will encompass service to the community.

This broadening of the scope would at first sight take the experience of the manufacturing industries even further away from applicability to the service sector. But in reality it makes no difference whatsoever to the fundamental premise. Manufacturing finally learnt that quality was only marginally impacted by technology and production techniques. The real root causes for failure were found to lie in the area of management, people and communication. These are exactly the same elements that exist in the service sector. After all, the service areas have made use of modern computer technology for a considerable time but their overall quality has not appreciably increased. In principle, therefore, the new management concepts apply equally to both sectors.

From the standpoint of achieving quality this book will argue that there are few differences in fundamental principles between the manufacturing and service sectors. It (politely) derides the oft-repeated argument of the service companies 'that we are different'.

The argument is that the problems encountered are so different in root cause from those of the production line, that there can be little affinity. Manufacturing companies learnt to apply the same principles with equal success to their own administrative and distribution areas. Comprehension of that experience led to the word 'total' being added as a prefix to the words 'quality management'.

Many service organisations are now beginning to prove the truth of these assertions. Each can learn from the others' experience in achieving world-class quality. Part One of this book describes the fundamental principles of quality management that can be shared by both sectors. It also describes the vision of total and continuous improvement that should be the objective of every organisation, whatever its purpose.

However, it is not quite so simple as the 'no difference' argument would appear to suggest. There are substantial differences in the application of the same fundamental principles. Paradoxically, the differences are rooted in the same concept that was used to argue the similarities: the concept that quality will be achieved through management, people and communication – in other words, by changing the culture of organisations, by changing the way people are managed and communicate with one another. But the culture of an organisation is dependent on the perceptions of people within the organisation. These perceptions are based on many factors, not least of which are industry traditions and practices. Perceptions become facts in living organisations because management and people react to one another and to situations on the basis of their perceptions. Organisational culture will differ between manufacturing companies and will surely differ between the service and manufacturing sectors. There will therefore be substantial differences between the implementation of cultural change for every unique organisation. The carpenter and the joiner use similar tools but they use them differently. Part Two of this book defines some of the important differences in perception and application that are present in various elements of the service sector.

'Making it Happen' is the heading for the third part of this book. It provides guidelines for those organisations that have made the decision to start on the journey towards Total Continuous Improvement. The chapters on providing and supporting the process describe the changes required in management behaviour to accomplish the desired change. The chapter 'Finding Joy in Work' describes the resulting change in the attitudes of all the employees. (These chapters combined describe the actions needed both to empower and to release the potential of employees and outline their impact.) The chapter 'Constancy of Purpose' discusses the problems involved in maintaining the initial impetus and keeping on course.

In essence, Part Four – 'Gathering up the Loose Ends' – is an appendix. It includes a brief description of the systems, tools and techniques of quality management available to assist the implementation process. Another chapter provides guidelines (possibly prejudiced) in selecting a consultant to help the organisation. A short chapter is included on 'Variation'. Executives in service organisations often have difficulty in seeing the concept of the reduction of variation as applying to their organisations. This chapter aims to remove that perception.

The final chapter, 'Stewardship – The Way Ahead', touches on some of the changes facing the world of managers over the next few years. They can be viewed as outside the main scope of this book but in reality no one change can be planned or implemented in isolation. So numerous are the changes about that only fools and managers dare contemplate them.

PART ONE

Principles For All

The common principles that can be
applied within any service organisation

2. WHAT IS TCI?

TCI, or Total and Continuous Improvement, is a strategic vision. It should be the objective for every organisation determined to meet the challenge of the future. TCI is a philosophy or way of life that can embrace management and people. It represents a customer-driven organisation in which every individual is part of a team continuously seeking to improve every element of its work – an organisation which sets its sights way beyond zero defects or the mere elimination of error. TCI is a vision that will release the potential of people for continuous improvement and innovation. An organisation which accepts TCI as the way we work will delight its customers and put the fun back into work for all its employees.

TCI is not to be confused with TQM, or Total Quality Management. One is an objective, the other is a management process. It is sometimes seen as yet another promotional mnemonic to replace TQM. In fact, both are valid and the author sees TCI as the objective for a TQM process. In that context TQM is not an objective at all. TQM is in reality the change agent or vehicle that is used to take the organisation on the journey from its present state to the destination of TCI.

Too many organisations have launched quality initiatives under the banner of TQM and a few years later suffered the disappointment that not much has really changed. Chapter 5 details the many reasons for such disappointment but argues that the primary reason for comparative failure is the lack of a real vision for the new endeavour. Quality on its own can be too constraining; TCI provides a vision for maintaining a constancy of purpose.

TCI and TQM are therefore different but also complementary. It is vital to understand the difference because they represent the difference between success and failure in the drive for quality. They also represent the difference between Japanese and much Western thinking on quality. This can be illustrated by examining the meaning of the words represented by the abbreviations.

Total Quality Management

TQM is the natural evolution of quality management. Quality was once seen as the province of manufacturing industry and even within that area concentrating on the production line. Quality assurance replaced inspection and then followed the realisation that the design and administrative processes were also contributors to quality or the lack of quality. Total quality was the phrase used to represent this change in perception. This was an important change in the evolution of quality for the service industries. When manufacturing industries began to use the same managerial concepts for the control of quality in their administrative areas they demonstrated that the concepts of quality management were equally applicable to service industries, which were mainly administrative. As a result a wide variety of service-oriented companies and public sector organisations are moving to TQM to improve their operations.

Those involved in TQM will all have their own precise definition of what is meant by the words 'total', 'quality' and 'management'. In the author's experience the majority would accept the following definitions:

In TQM the word *total* recognises that every individual in the organisation must contribute to the complete service now demanded by the customer. In other words, the customer evaluates the organisation's performance by more than the prime service provided. In that context the time taken to process a proposal or a claim for insurance is probably more important than the financial factors. The hospital patient is probably more concerned about the waiting list, the method of admission and the standard of the outpatients' waiting room than the quality of surgery, which he tends to take for granted. In other words, the use of the word 'total' is meant to emphasise the extension from the 'production line', or the main product, to every element of the business.

The word *quality* is used to emphasise a number of concepts though it obviously indicates the evolutionary source of the concepts. For the majority of people quality is a subjective term such as 'luxury' or 'top of the market'. On that basis individuals will have their own view of what constitutes quality, which would make it impossible to manage because no two individuals in the organisation could agree that it had been achieved.

TQM recognises that there has to be a common objective definition for quality that everyone in the organisation will accept: a definition which leaves no room for doubt about whether it is or is not being achieved and one that cannot be fudged or avoided. There are several definitions for quality used by TQM adherents which meet these criteria. *Fitness for use* and *conformance to requirements* are the most common definitions but the author believes that today's marketplace demands a more exacting definition – for example, 'delighting the customer by continually meeting and improving upon agreed requirements'. The real point is that these definitions provide a measurable context to quality and widen the scope beyond the prime product or service.

The word *management* highlights the point that quality as defined above will not be achieved by accident. When one individual was responsible for the totality of the product – the era of the craftsmen – quality was a natural result of pride and personal identification. This is rarely the case today. The complexity of modern business involves a large number of people in the delivery of a complete service to the customer. Achieving quality in those conditions demands a managed process – a recognition that even the smallest work activity is part of a chain of processes linked together to provide the overall service.

Comprehension of these issues can involve a major cultural change in the organisation. Because we have ignored these factors in the past we have created an environment of management behaviour and employee attitudes which actually work against the achievement of quality. TQM therefore is a management process which recognises that quality is achieved through people. More important, it also states that the workers will only be able to achieve quality if management comprehends the issues and helps the people with systems and tools designed to measure and communicate the problems they are facing.

The author emphasises that this is a very short summary of what is involved in the concept of TQM. There is a substantial library of books on the subject, of which his own *Global Quality – The New Management Culture* is only a minor part.

Management perception of quality

For most service organisations the achievement of TCI will demand a fundamental change in management's perception of quality. Lest this statement is seen as yet another tirade against modern management we also need to understand the historical background to those perceptions. Therefore before embarking on the full meaning of TCI it is worth considering the source of the traditional management attitude to quality.

Since the beginning of this century management has been conditioned by the subdivision of manufacturing activities to allow mass production. One impact of that change was that the individual worker or craftsman was no longer responsible for the totality of the product. That of course was the intention but it also meant that the individual was no longer responsible for the quality of the final product. In this environment, management's task was to drive, motivate or incentivise (for example, by piece-work rates) the worker to produce ever higher numbers, in a given time, of their minute component of the total product. The workers responded to this stimulation (not necessarily willingly) and mass production was proven as the new manufacturing culture. Certainly mass production did provide massive benefits, not only to the factory owners, but to society as a whole as represented by consumers.

It would be wrong to assume that factory managers were no longer interested in the quality of the final product. They wholly understood that their customers, albeit having the opportunity to purchase products they previously never dreamed of owning, still required that their purchases actually worked. Having taken away the individual responsibility for overall quality, new ways had to be devised to satisfy the vast numbers of new customers. Thus began the era of inspection. Cadres of the very best workers were selected to inspect all the manufactured components and to identify and isolate all the 'bad' items. Some of those items, already manufactured, were totally rejected and others were scheduled for 'rework'.

The inspection route to quality spawned deep-rooted perceptions about the organisation of work which have passed down through generations of managers and still persist today. The most damaging aspects of this conventional wisdom are that managers believe that the achievement of quality improvement is an expensive addition to the production process and that the workers are not interested in quality. One of the themes of this book is that both these perceptions are wrong.

Inspection-based quality *is* an expensive process. This way improved quality comes from increasing the number of inspectors or the inspection levels. The measure of performance becomes the height of the rejection pile or the volume in the rework bays. A pristine new factory will include rework areas in the design layout. In other words, the factory managers have planned to manufacture bad goods from the outset. In their minds this is the way work has to be.

With hindsight we now know how expensive this approach to production can be. A conservative estimate proven over and over again is that the real cost of all this bad quality is in excess of 25 per cent of sales revenue. Just imagine Chippendale being prepared to throw away one in every four chairs he had so lovingly laboured over. But this is exactly what the mass production management practices had achieved. Now we have to return to the standards of the original craftsmen and so organise our work that every process is completed right first time.

So what about the position of the craftsmen – or, as we now call them, workers, employees or 'our people' – in the organisation of work? The ethos of mass production has taken the average operative further and further away from the final product of their labour: 'We are no longer responsible for quality, so why should we care? In any case it would be unfair to the inspectors if we didn't give them some bad components to find.' Management's concern about increased production at the expense of everything else merely strengthened this attitude. Measurement and people appraisal systems concentrated on numbers or volume of production and rarely quality. If management were declaring 'never mind the quality, feel the width' what else could the workers do? But managers extended this approach into a perception that this was also the way the workers viewed quality – that bad quality was really the result of an uncaring workforce rather than the result of their own management practices. Now we have to release the caring potential – the pride of people.

It is interesting that the management of service industries have inherited the same conventional wisdom. They are so fond of saying 'but we are different from manufacturing' that they do not recognise they are often applying the same outdated management practices. Indeed, it is worse than that because over the last decade manufacturing management have become unblinkered and are working hard to change. The organisation of work is about people, communication and management – not machines or technology. Those conditions apply equally to service as to manufacturing industry.

In fairness, most modern managers of service industries do recognise the customer-driven imperative for improved quality, but they find it difficult to comprehend the changes demanded in their own behaviour. Executives and managers of service organisations are not fools or 'trouble at 't mill' traditionalists. (However, the author has worked with a service industry client who had four levels of toilet, three levels of canteen and operational rules which prevented promotion to departmental manager until the age of thirty-five. It should also be said that this same company by its own efforts has achieved the most dramatic change of culture the author has witnessed, and in as little as two years.)

In the author's experience the majority of these managers recognise that their greatest asset is their people and genuinely want to encourage teamwork and participation. They spend a considerable amount of time and money trying to improve communication within their organisations. They read books, attend conferences and seek external advice. Unfortunately, for many the plethora of ideas, concepts and techniques presented only create confusion. The teachings of the quality gurus and their adherents has opened a Pandora's box of concepts that appear to threaten all perceived management wisdom. The aim of this book is to remove the confusion and to provide a new vision called TCI.

The vision

Every organisation which wants to unite its workforce and provide horizons for thought and action amongst its executives requires a vision: a sense of purpose – a combined sense of purpose in what we are trying to achieve. The first essential element of the vision is a statement defining the business purpose of the organisation, or what Americans call a Mission Statement. The second element of the vision is a definition of the principles and values by which we are going to achieve our business purpose – or in less pompous terms, the shared agreement on how we are going to work together as a team to achieve the purpose. Only those with responsibility for the overall direction of the organisation can define the purpose. TCI aims to support the second element of the vision: the way we are going to work together.

In his role as a consultant the author always asks the senior management team: 'Do you have a purpose or mission statement?' Increasingly the answer is an unequivocal 'yes'. The next question is: 'Do you also have a set of principles and values to support the purpose statement?' At this point there is generally a little doubt. A likely result from the ensuing discussion is that the Personnel or Human Relations Director will sum up by saying something like: 'Well yes, we do have principles contained in our policies and we are working on a complete statement for our employees.' This is an interesting answer because it easily prompts the next question from the consultant: 'Do all your employees know exactly what is contained within the Mission Statement and the supporting principles and values?' The answer to this is usually predictable. The executives look at each other and one will mention that they are included in the procedures manual,or: 'Oh, yes, there was a special page in the staff newsletter.' The third inevitable question will usually receive an unequivocal 'No' and that is: 'Does every employee understand the changes required to really make those principles and values come alive?'

The whole of this fairly typical discourse illustrates the need for a complete vision which is understood by everyone in the organisation. TCI is part of that vision.

Total Continuous Improvement

TCI is a philosophy of management: a new management culture in which everyone in the organisation is working together to achieve the same overall purpose. Developed to the full it is almost a political philosophy which could end the ceaseless hassle between management and workers. Some Japanese companies have moved a long way down the road to TCI and have their own word, *Kaizen*, to represent their approach. Western organisations could take the philosophy further but it will entail a fundamental change in management behaviour. Its successful adoption will bring an equally fundamental change in the attitudes of all employees.

These are major claims and the reader is entitled to some explanation as to why the author considers them to be a philosophy rather than just another management fad. In common with a host of other managers, over the last thirty years the author had jumped on a variety of bandwagons heralded as the complete answer to management problems. These included MBO (management by objectives), TA (transactional analysis) and more recently time management. Most have had some value but were found wanting as a philosophy of management.

Earlier TQM was described by examining the meaning of its individual words and a similar method can be used to describe the philosophy of TCI. This will also help to differentiate the change agent from the objective of the change.

The word *total* in TCI encompasses much wider horizons. At the start of the process of change the focus tends to be internal to the organisation. The emphasis is on ensuring understanding by all that the efficient running of the organisation depends on the interdependence of every individual and every function in the delivery of product and service. In TQM the word quality is used to provide the external focus on delighting the customer. Once that comprehension has been achieved the word 'total' takes on a wider significance – a realisation that management also involves a series of interdependencies outside the organisation.

A TCI-motivated management will certainly ensure that everyone is involved in the achievement of the organisational purpose. They will also wholly understand that the customer is at the centre of that purpose. It will be a customer-driven organisation. However, the management will also recognise in the word 'total' even wider responsibilities and spheres of influence. Such an organisation will actively seek to bring its suppliers into the fold of the family or, more prosaically, ensure that the external suppliers share identity with the overall *common* purpose. Furthermore, it will recognise that it shares a level of responsibility for society as a whole, is part of that society and must take proper account of the community at large and the environment in its decision criteria. Suffice to say at this stage that the word 'total' as used here covers a wider spectrum than would be recognised from the routine actions of most executives.

The word *continuous* in TCI has a number of connotations which primarily reflect that management is a living process rather than just a programme of specific actions. Its meaning emanates from the teaching of the statisticians (primarily Deming) who command us to measure the continuous performance of a process over time so that we can predict its capability as a prerequisite for improvement actions. This is in contradiction to the conventional management impulse to take immediate action and tinker with isolated aspects of the process without understanding its overall behaviour. In that context the TCI organisation is a capable process working within control limits. As a philosophy it is perhaps better expressed as 'this is the way we work around here'. All the concepts of improvement are in the woodwork of the organisation. The organisation fully understands its behaviour so it can continuously seek to improve itself in a rational manner. This is in contradiction to the stop-go lurches common in industry (and government), which during the author's experience of the fast-moving computer industry were called the 'October Revolution'.

Improvement is a word that appears to speak for itself, but once again it is a word that has many interpretations in the world of quality improvement. A philosophy of course is about interpretation, so let's be clear what improvement means under the banner of TCI.

The alumni of the Philip Crosby Quality Colleges would primarily interpret improvement as the elimination of error in all our work processes. The achievement of zero defects is a laudable objective and surely a major step forward for most organisations. However, many Deming adherents argue that chasing zero defects is a pointless exercise as the real objective is to ensure that processes are in control so that the organisation can concentrate on reducing the variation present in all work activities. In other words, even when every defect has been eliminated there is still a massive opportunity for improvement.

Having worked in both environments and having a high personal regard for both gurus the author wonders what the argument is all about. TCI recognises that an individual performance standard that will not tolerate error, and indeed views error as an opportunity for improvement, is a powerful force in any organisation. An organisation operating in the TCI culture would see no contradiction in utilising that same force to seek to reduce variation in all its work processes. Both of these approaches represent continuous improvement.

So TCI embraces two common strains of thought in quality improvement but it also has a higher and to some extent more exciting objective. The world-class TCI organisation not only involves all its people in improvements but it seeks to release their infinite potential for innovative and creative thought. That is an objective fit for nations, let alone individual companies.

Releasing the potential of people has become a management catch phrase but few operating managers have really understood its significance. Toyota, for example, claim to receive one million suggestions every year from their workforce. *One million per year.* In terms of most organisations that is a mind-boggling statistic. Let's bring this down to more manageable proportions by comparing two organisations in Britain rather than Japan – both real but will remain anonymous here.

Company A is in the financial services sector and has close to twenty-thousand employees. It operates a traditional corporate suggestions system. Company B is a manufacturing company with little over two thousand employees. It involves those employees in improvement and innovation teams. Look at the comparative results:

	Company A	Company B
Number of employees	20,000	2,300
Suggestions received	474	3,600
Suggestions implemented	27	3,100

Which company is really releasing the potential of its people? The implication and lessons to be learned from those figures will be developed in Chapter 19 (Finding Joy in Work), but two comments are worth making at this stage. Company B operates in the North-East of England and a large proportion of its employees previously worked in the mining and shipbuilding industries. Neither of those industries were exactly famous for the close working collaboration between management and workers.

So something has happened in Company B to change traditional attitudes and working relationships. Management has changed its behaviour and the workers have as a result changed their attitudes. This goes to the heart of the TCI process. Lest the reader draw the wrong implication between service and manufacturing businesses it should be noted that Company A is now well down the TQM stage and last year reported 571 separate quality initiatives from one department alone.

This chapter has attempted to start a comprehension of the philosophy behind Total Continuous Improvement. It has included the constant repetition of the words culture, behaviour and attitudes. Even with the above examples this could lead the reader to consider that TCI is a nice idea but has little practical application in the real business world. The author once thought this but he has been converted by watching the change in action.

A strong word of warning. The term 'consensus management' is being widely used in the West to describe Japanese management practices and, by implication, the philosophy of TCI. The attempted application of the Western understanding of this term is a very dangerous concept which can lead to a total abdication of management responsibility. Quite apart from the fact that it would not work it is a travesty of what is really happening in Japan.

Japanese executives will certainly seek facts and opinions from a much wider spectrum than their Western counterparts. They will be particularly interested in the views of those who will be most involved in executing the resultant decision. Such executives have an inherent belief that most business decisions are worth pondering and have no concerns that they are exhibiting weakness by giving time to the decision. It is, of course, a slower process than the traditional Western code of instant or 'authoritative' decision-making. However, Japanese executives are not seeking the 'lowest common denominator' or a majority decision. In that sense they are not seeking consensus but the right decision – and they will make that decision.

The next action of Japanese executives will be even further from the practice of traditional Western executives. They will explain the reasoning behind the decision to those responsible for its execution so that there is a high level of commitment to achieving success. At that stage they will not countenance objection or obstruction.

This process is not consensus as now being propounded by some consultants. The author is a strong advocate of involving people in the decision-making process. By experience he has found that the practice is a powerful stimulant to lateral thought. However, he is still traditional enough to believe that you always need an odd number to make decisions and that three is usually too many.

3. DO WE NEED TCI?

A typical executive (if there is such an animal), if asked the question 'Do we need TQM or TCI in our company?', might well ponder. The pondering could be along the following lines. We are a successful organisation and recognised as leaders in our field. We do value our customers and recognise that our success is dependent on our people. We have good and well-trained managers who work hard to improve communication and to develop teamwork in the organisation. We also know that we are operating in a changing world and that change has to be managed, but to add another change for its own sake could be destructive. Why change a winning formula? So do we really need to embark on this journey to TCI? The easy empirical answer is yes; and if you do not you may not survive the nineties. However, that answer is just a little too simple for most executives.

In reality each organisation has to decide the answer for itself. What can be said is that conventional management practices create an awesome level of wasted resources, mostly involved in fire-fighting, reworking and frustrating breakdowns in communication. The evidence is overwhelming. In the manufacturing industries those who started out on the quality revolution generally found that the level of wasted resource amounted to some 25 per cent of their sales revenue. More recently the service industries have found that the level of waste generally exceeds 30 per cent of their operating costs.

These examples – proved over and over again – are not drawn from companies who would be considered failures in the competitive market place. World-class companies such as ICI, IBM, 3M, Sheraton Hotels and Prudential Assurance would attest to similar figures before they started the quest for quality.

The evidence also shows that these figures are equally true for large corporations and relatively small organisations. Yet before exposure to TQM most executives believe that the level of waste in their own organisation probably does not exceed six to ten per cent.

It would surprise them to know that even these figures would horrify the typical Japanese executive.

These horrendous costs are only one factor to consider in viewing the total effectiveness or capability of the organisation to meet the future with confidence. They represent the cost of bad quality internally and the remedial costs of trying to achieve acceptable external quality. As such, these costs are only symptoms of how the organisation operates. In their own right they obviously impact the manoeuvrability of the management in the fields of pricing strategy, promotion and investment. They put the future at risk. But the very same breakdowns in communication, firefighting and rework that created this level of wasted resource within the organisation also have other crucial side-effects.

The same root causes contribute to failures or delays in service and provoke the annoyance and frustration of customers. The missed standing order, the delayed issuance of an insurance policy or the postponed hip operation are other symptoms of the same misuse of resources. Again the future is at risk. As soon as a competitor proves that it can alleviate these customer frustrations on a continuing basis your customers are gone – perhaps for ever. The evidence for this abounds in the USA and Europe since the advent of the new quality revolution from Japan. On a different comparative scale it is now being proven once again in Eastern Europe. The disappearance of once famous brand names, the collapse of whole industries and, on the national scale, growing trade deficits are all evidence of conventional and outdated managerial practices.

Productivity and service quality are not different issues to be tackled separately. They are two sides of the same coin. At the extreme many organisations are in a vicious circle; like a dog chasing its own tail. The continual repetition of the same unresolved problems (most individually fairly small) and bad-tempered customers frustrate and depress the morale of employees. Powerless to change the situation, they no longer care and just look forward to closing time. This attitude increases the level of error, bad service and cost. Faced with falling margins and declining sales, management stamps hard on the brake with cost-cutting and lay-offs. The vicious circle has begun to spin faster and sooner or later the bearings will go and the organisation will have begun the final spin.

These disastrous results of conventional management practices are all too common in service organisations. The author has not resorted to hyperbole. However, most managers would want more evidence of these 'outdated practices' before accepting that any of them apply to their operations. In considering the evidence it is essential to understand that the author is not focusing on wicked, bad or merely weak managers. The intention is to castigate the management process rather than the individual managers.

Conventional practices are the result of conventional training and the conventional operating environment in which the manager gains his experience. Good managers have been wrestling with these environmental constraints over a long period. For years organisations successfully operated within common conventions and there was, therefore, no imperative to challenge them. As long as everyone was working to the same rules all was well. But the Japanese were forced to start again and this helps the examination of basic principles. They listened to profound knowledge (from Dr Deming and others) and as a result started with a new set of conventional rules. The service industries have only just begun to be challenged by the new game plan and are thus perhaps behind their manufacturing brethren. TQM and TCI are all about the new conventions to be learned.

Deep at the heart of TCI is a new comprehension of the nature of work, the nature and behaviour of people and the role of management in maximising the potential of both. The achievement of TCI requires a fundamental change in management behaviour which can only start with an understanding of the good business reasons to change. The effects of present management thinking were noted earlier in this chapter but by themselves these do not provide many clues as to what has to change. They should have created a desire to investigate the need to change.

From whatever perspective that we choose to look at the nature of organisations we are faced with one inescapable fact. Managers control resources. Whether they should or shouldn't doesn't really matter: the fact is that they do and always have done, whatever the nature of the human organisation. It is equally true for religious, political or business organisations, whatever their fundamental principles. The cardinal in an autocratic religion, the apparatchik in a communist state, the gauleiter in a fascist state, the council leader in a democratic socialist system and the executive in a market-oriented capitalist system all share one thing in common: their control of resources. Each of these ethics may establish constraints on the use of these resources, which could vary from the ten commandments to consumer demand. In each arena there will also be policing systems to enforce the constraints. The inquisition, the commissar, the gestapo or even consumer legislation immediately come to mind.

From a business perspective the intriguing issue is that the arguments about the ownership or the constraints often blind management to the fact of – and even more often to the responsibility for – control. If they fully comprehended the nature of the work which stems from this control of resources they would not be endlessly blaming their people for the misuse of resources. Management can coerce, motivate or incentivise people to increase productivity, improve quality and be nice to customers, but unless they understand the meaning of the control of resources their maximum effectiveness is unlikely to exceed twenty per cent of the potential improvement. The ability to eliminate error, the ability to reduce variation, the ability to release innovation and the power of people are all directly related to management's control and sharing of the resources that they alone command. At least we should have learned this from totalitarian dictatorships.

To better understand this relationship between management and people let's forget the grand social or historical issues and concentrate on the nature of work. All work is a process of converting or transforming a series of inputs into a different output or set of outputs. The aim of every business is to manage the process of transformation so that it will provide sufficient added value both to pay for the conversion and to provide a profit. This is as true of manufacturing as of service industries. In one case steel, wood, leather and a myriad of previously manufactured parts are transformed into a motor car. In another case an individual proposal form for life assurance can be converted into a profitable guarantee that the individual's dependants are protected in the event of death or injury. Of course this simple definition of the purpose of organisations becomes more complex in practice. Neither of these examples is completed in one simple process. Each of these conversions entail a whole series of connected processes to complete the transformation. Clearly the steel will require moulding to shape in one process, the wood and leather cut and worked to shape in another and all assembled together in another. In the service example the age and medical records included on the insurance proposal form will require separate computations for risk in separate processes and both will need to be 'assembled' into an insurance policy. In other words, both manufacturing and service businesses require the organisation and management of a large number of individual work processes.

In quality terms these linked processes have often been referred to as the 'process chain' and the analogy has been drawn that the chain is only as strong as the weakest link. This is a reasonable analogy to illustrate the point that final product or service quality depends on the contribution of many functions within the organisation. It is a good starting point for comprehension of some of the communication problems that exist in the nature of work. However, it is too simplistic to provide real comprehension of the issues facing management. The cell structure of a beehive comes nearer to illustrating what is actually happening in a business. A structure in which every cell is dependent on the strength of a host of other independent cells. Some of these complexities will be examined in the chapters of Part Two. Management confusion about the exercise of the control of resources is in part created by the complexity of interrelationships but at root it is caused by a basic misunderstanding of the simple requirements of the simplest process cell.

The simple process diagram illustrated in Figure 1 describes what happens in the smallest cell of a major process. At this level the suppliers and customers of the process are likely to be internal. For the large majority of workers the customer to be delighted is a colleague rather than the final customer. In this situation the inputs to this process are likely to be outputs from another internal process and similarly the outputs from this process are likely to be the inputs for yet another process. This diagram is helpful up to a point in illustrating what is happening but it misses some essential elements. To operate the process a number of constraints or requirements must be defined so that the people working in the process can have a clear idea of what is expected of them. This is where the management misunderstanding of the power of the people to improve begins.

Figure 2 shows the same diagram expanded to include a series of requirements in the process and represents a relatively simple process – typing a letter. The customer, or output requirements, should drive the whole process. When these have been defined and agreed it is possible to establish requirements on the supplier. For example, if the typed letter is required by 15.30 hours then the draft (meeting its other requirements) is required no later than 15.00 hours. It is interesting that in this process the prime customer and supplier are the same individual, namely the manager. In that relationship it is amusing to reflect on how often all the supplier's requirements are met! But there are some other requirements which are vital to the continuous performance of the process: the ever present requirements of the process itself and the resources required by the people working in the process.

Even in this simple process we can begin to see the problems facing the people working in the process or, in this case, the typist. For the typist to meet all of the customer requirements every time the input and process requirements must also be met every time. Yet the typist has little or no control over the provision of those resources. It is very difficult to provide an error-free letter if the draft is illegible. If the typewriter provided by management does not have a 'Century Schoolbook typeface' that requirement cannot be met. Most critical of all, if the procedures and required layouts are

Figure 1.
Simple process diagram

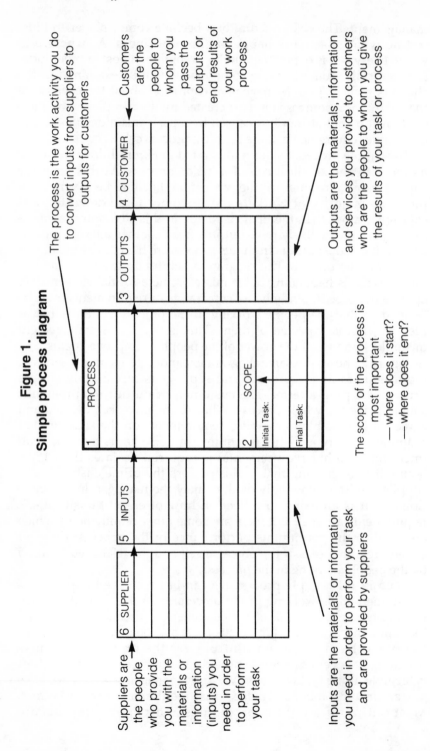

The process is the work activity you do to convert inputs from suppliers to outputs for customers

Customers are the people to whom you pass the outputs or end results of your work process

Outputs are the materials, information and services you provide to customers who are the people to whom you give the results of your task or process

The scope of the process is most important
— where does it start?
— where does it end?

Suppliers are the people who provide you with the materials or information (inputs) you need in order to perform your task

Inputs are the materials or information you need in order to perform your task and are provided by suppliers

Figure 2.
A simple process

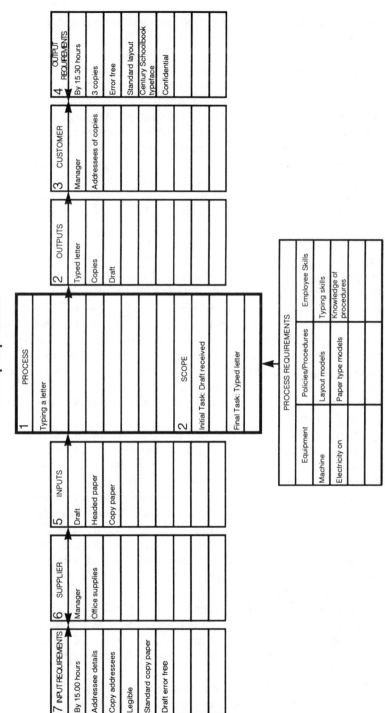

unclear and the typist has not been trained in their use, the 'standard layout' requirement is unlikely to be met.

Unclear requirements are not only unfair to the worker: they are the largest single cause of error and waste. The real lesson to be learned from this exercise is that the major proportion of the resources and requirements for the process is under the control of managers rather than workers. The people working in the process are almost powerless to improve the process without help from management. No amount of motivation or admonitions to achieve zero defects are of any use at all unless management recognise their role in work processes. Managers must learn to understand the process, listen to the people working in the process as they explain the problems they are encountering and then collaborate and *help* the workers improve the process.

Even a simple process can be used to illustrate some of the problems implicit in organising work. In real life the issue is more complicated if not complex. Figures 3 and 4 are examples of forms used to analyse the flow and network relationships in a large-scope process made up of many simple-scope processes. These could be used to define the relationship and number of processes required to provide and charge for a rental car from the first request by a customer. Equally, the same approach could be used to analyse the processes required to organise elective bed admissions to a hospital. Each of the resource, requirements and communications issues noted in the simple example of typing a letter is multiplied at every interface in the network.

There is another factor which compounds the problem and tends to obscure all of this activity from management attention. Business schools and experience have taught executives to concentrate their attention on the 'significant few' issues and to ignore the 'insignificant many'. On the face of it that sounds eminently sensible, but it has one flaw. It automatically assumes that someone else, a supervisor or worker, is looking after the insignificant many. They are not. This is not because they do not want to or are being 'bloody-minded'. They have simply not been empowered with the resources to solve all these little problems. They are continually trying to bring management's attention to these issues but they are not significant enough to interest management. It is only when all the little problems mount up to a major catastrophe, such as the loss of a major order, that they reach the executive's threshold of pain and something is done. Meanwhile all the insignificant people go on living and working in pain.

A large proportion of the waste noted earlier in this chapter comes from hundreds of insignificant problems which are repeated

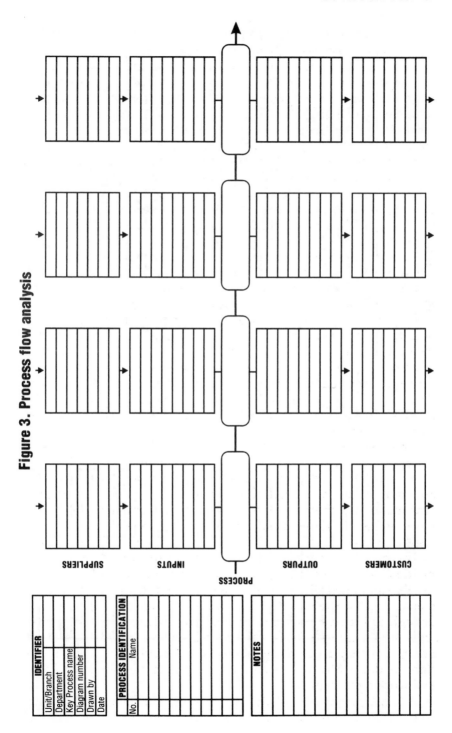

Figure 3. Process flow analysis

Figure 4. Key process network diagram

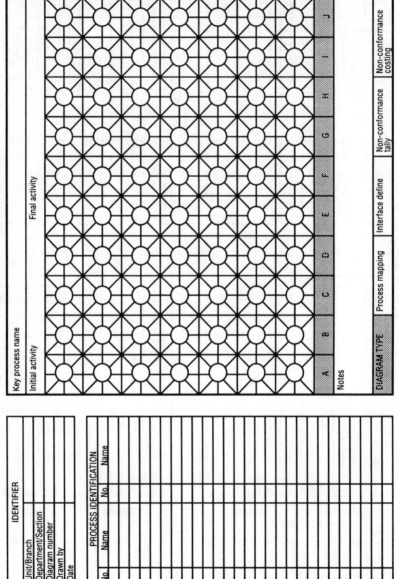

over and over again. They are just not recognised as existing at this cumulative value. In the author's view thirty per cent of operating costs should be enough to cross any executive's threshold of pain!

Customers are also funny about small problems. More quality reputations are lost over a host of little issues than the one major defect. Consider two purchasers of cars. Each takes home the new model proudly to demonstrate to family and friends their excitement with all the new features. Customer A's car performs well until about four weeks after purchase it develops a major defect in the gearbox. The car has to be towed away to the service station and major repairs are needed. It is all put right in a few days at no cost to the customer but he is naturally annoyed. A year later nothing else has gone wrong and he is asked about his satisfaction with the car. 'Oh, a few teething problems but they were soon put right and in my opinion it was a great buy.'

Customer B's car develops no major faults at all and for some months he is a delighted customer. Then little faults begin to appear; one door does not lock on the central locking system, a knob keeps falling off when taking a left-hand bend – nothing serious and the knob can be put back on. A few little things not quite important enough to face the inconvenience of putting the car into the service station for a couple of days. The service station would gladly repair these little problems on warranty at no charge but they get ignored. Customer B, asked the same question a year later, will probably start to mutter about Friday cars and the company reputation for quality has taken a plunge. The insignificant many have triumphed again.

Much of what has been discussed in this chapter relates to management comprehension and attitudes. It is this lack of real understanding of the nature of work and of the reasons for the workers' behaviour that has allowed the conventional management practices to endure. Even good and caring managers fall into the trap of using practices which actually compound rather than alleviate the problems. Almost every issue with quality stems from management behaviour and the resultant attitude of the employees. It is all about communication in the work place.

There are three fundamental management practices which contribute to the confusion and waste in the organisation. They all arise from outdated views of what actually happens in the workplace and can be summarised as:

- Organising and setting objectives on a functional rather than a process basis.
- An obsession with the measurement of people rather than processes.

- Reluctance to empower people with the resources and permission to take action.

Each of these areas will be developed in detail in Part Three (Making It Happen). The reader who still has doubts about whether his organisation needs to start the journey to TCI should try to answer the following questions:

- Do you always delight your customers?
- Do you ever have customer complaints?
- Do the same customers always come back to you or is it an endless battle to find new customers?
- Do you really know what your customer wants now and in the future?

Some more questions to ask of the organisation:

- Does everyone view error as an opportunity for improvement?
- Does the organisation shoot the messenger – or do we use phrases such as 'Jim is negative – he gives me problems not solutions'?
- Is everyone committed to delighting the customer – internal or external?
- Is everyone free of fear or anxiety so that they readily and truthfully communicate their problems to their management?
- Does everyone enjoy their work?
- Does everyone share a common vision?

If you are still doubtful, a qualified consultant can help you assess the true position of your organisation in the competitive world.

4. IS IT WORTH ALL THE TROUBLE?

The opening chapters should have instilled into the reader some desire to change and even a recognition that there is a need to make some changes in their own organisation. However, they will also have brought a realisation that the changes being argued are radical. The whole change process is beginning to emerge as more difficult to achieve than appeared at the outset. Despite a desire to change the question still hovers – 'We are doing okay at the moment; is the resulting upheaval really worth all the trouble?'

The benefits claimed for the TQM approach are so enormous that they may sound like a confidence trick. They represent the impossible business dream – a total win-win situation. The claims are so great that it would be folly to ignore them. The sceptical reader should ask himself the question: how did the Japanese perform their economic miracle? Remember that less than forty years ago their products were a shoddy mimicry of Western goods. They had no natural resources. They were geographically further away from the prime markets than their competitors. They used even more autocratic management methods than their Western competition. There were some attitudes in their society that helped but it was not a totally compliant workforce. No, they looked at the way work was traditionally organised and decided to change their management culture. The results are self-evident.

One of the barriers to an easy acceptance of the new management culture does stem from our perception of the Japanese and their culture. It fascinates the Westerner but still seems alien to our own culture and attitudes. Of course, this does hark back to history and in particular the Second World War, but not totally. This view could also apply to Germany but most executives have easily freed their minds from such encumbrances in their relations with German businessmen. The same executives still feel that the differences between their own and the Japanese working culture are so great that there are few practical lessons to be learnt or imported. However, they do not have to rely on studying Japanese workers to provide the example. There are several Japanese companies operating in the USA and the UK who demonstrate the same lessons. None of them employ Japanese workers and indeed most of them are managed by Western managers. They may be implementing Japanese methods but they are doing it in a Western culture with Western managers and workers. Though the majority of the prime examples are in manufacturing we are just beginning to experience the same approach in service industries.

This growing experience is teaching the West something else from which they can derive both hope and confidence. Many Japanese companies based in the West, employing indigenous labour and management, are outperforming the equivalent operations in Japan. In other words, if we are prepared to understand and embrace Japanese management practices the released potential of our people can outstrip the Japanese workers. Our own long history of differing values has developed an inherent creativity that has an advantage when compared with the intense rote-based education of the Japanese. The barrier is not culture but old-fashioned willpower. We need to free ourselves from the obscurantism of our national myopias and view these management practices in a clear light.

Many American and European businesses totally free of any Japanese influence have seen the light and adopted the principles of TQM and TCI. They have emerged as world-class performers in their own right. We are really considering a global change in management culture.

A word of caution before we get too euphoric. The benefits of TCI are enormous for any organisation but they do not grant a divine immunity from all the exigent requirements for success. A TCI environment will not automatically ensure that the major marketing, technology or other strategic decisions are sound. Even a TCI company can be threatened by the emergence of a new technology or a fundamental shift in demand. When we discuss the interdependencies of processes within the organisation we must never forget the external dimension. Government policies, international emergencies (remember the impact of the Gulf War on the leisure and tourist industries) and the actions of other companies are all external interdependencies that impact the performance of the organisation. Hopefully a TCI company is more likely to develop the antennae to recognise these shifts earlier and will be more flexible in reacting. Nevertheless, the entrepreneurial spirit and the challenge of decision-making is still an essential element in success.

Specific examples of the benefits of the TCI approach will appear throughout this book. For the purposes of this chapter the benefits of the successful implementation of the culture change can be summarised as:

- Greatly improved product or service.
- A major reduction in wasted resources.
- A massive leap in productivity.
- The best opportunity, available to most, to increase margins and bottom-line profit.
- Ability to compress the time to design, build and launch new products – in other words, reacting to the market place.
- A long-term increase in market share.
- A sustained competitive advantage.
- A real release of the potential of the workforce.
- A motivated workforce.

And finally a WIIFM (what's in it for me) for the executive and the manager with the courage to make the change: they can look forward to the elimination of much of the hassle and frustration involved in managing an organisation.

5. DOES IT ALWAYS WORK?

The drive for quality improvement is not new. Since the late seventies thousands of Western companies have woken up to the challenge from the Far East and launched some form of quality initiative. As a result many have become world-class competitors. The success of companies such as 3M, Xerox, ICI, Compaq and Milliken has been well documented and much can be learnt from their experience. Unfortunately it is also true that many organisations have not met with the same measure of success. We can also learn from their experiences.

Success is a comparative term. Some of the unsuccessful companies would have difficulty in admitting failure. To some extent this demonstrates the natural human tendency to trumpet success and to hide failure; few companies are prepared to reveal the blot on the escutcheon. In truth the measure of success for them is somewhere in between. This view is understandable for, almost without exception, every company that has launched a quality drive has improved. In business terms quality has been in focus and has shown a positive return – therefore it has been successful. But the real measure of success should be against competitors and the expectations at the outset, i.e. the expectations of those who initiated the drive to be a quality leader. Seen in that light many companies have some reasons for disappointment.

The author's experience and research have led him to recognise nine principal reasons for disappointment. These are summarised as follows:

- Lack of management commitment.
- Lack of vision and planning.
- Satisfaction with the quick fix.
- The process became tool-bound.
- Quality too constraining.
- Culture change versus project approach.
- Quality management became institutionalised.

- The people were not really involved.
- Lack of real business measurables.

Each of these reasons for disappointment or traps for the unwary will be developed in this chapter. But as a useful illustrative diversion it may be worthwhile to examine the author's original experience and therefore his own comparative measurement base.

Though he can never claim to be a conceptual pioneer, for he relied on others' original and profound thought, the author was an early practical pioneer in the quality revolution; starting in the foothills, he had only limited experience to guide him. As he climbed the mountain he either made or flirted with every mistake possible on the track to TCI. But there has proved to be one advantage to those early travails. He was not alone; from the outset he has developed a contact network of other practical pioneers which has been maintained and extended. We all need each other's help. This worldwide collaboration still provides a reservoir of experience and thought. It also has to be admitted that he was not struck by blinding truth on the road to Damascus. He was led to re-evaluate his premises by the harsh circumstances of business survival. In other words, he can share a similar route to conversion that he is now preaching to other managers.

His company was evaluating what appeared to be trial marketing by the Japanese into the computer market (at that time he was UK Director of Strategic and Product Marketing in an international computer company). The survival shock was totally unexpected. The Japanese were not attempting to enter the market with cheap copies of Western computers, as might have been expected. They intended to compete with state-of-the-art products and price them at 108 per cent of IBM parity, the then industry competitive pricing standard. Worse, they intended to charge only 25 per cent of the then standard industry maintenance price. But the real sting in the tail was that an independent survey showed that if the company reduced its maintenance charges by 75 per cent the customers would be scared stiff and rush to third-party maintenance companies to provide service security. The survey also showed that the same customers had no such fears with the Japanese products and apparently readily accepted their reliability claims. In other words, the customers' perception of Japanese quality was that it was above that of the leading American companies. In some industries these could have been just perception shocks but in those days the mainframe computer industry depended on maintenance revenue for profit. This therefore was a real survival issue and quality rapidly became a major corporate priority. The expectation or target for quality improvement was set at a very high level.

In summation, to continue the mountaineering analogy, the author has looked over the precipice. He has stared the cost of failure in the face. He knows by experience that the price of constructing a road to the top of the mountain is not cheap but in the long term it is worth every penny. The nine following reasons for disappointment should be viewed as warnings of rockfalls above, all of which can be circumvented.

1. Lack of management commitment

The most frequent reason advanced for the comparative failure of quality initiatives is a lack of management commitment to see the process through. The disillusioned comments can be paraphrased as: 'We got off to a good start, the staff were all for it but somehow it all petered out – management didn't stay committed.' Quality had been seen as the 'flavour of the year' and now the organisation had a new flavour. In other words, quality improvement had been treated as a short-term programme rather than as a never-ending process.

In reality this is a too simplistic excuse and does not go the root cause of failure. It was not commitment but comprehension that was lacking. Commitment is another modern management in-word or cop-out. It is a word beloved of sales and marketing management. Commitment is a relatively easy motivational response to achieve at the beginning of any programme. It can be achieved at a Nuremberg rally or at most management meetings if called for by the boss. After all, who can really be against quality. The real issue is that management generally had little understanding as to what they were supposed to be committed to. At any stage of the programme the management would have considered themselves committed to quality and been delighted to have made another rabble-rousing speech to demonstrate their commitment.

Earlier chapters showed that the road to TCI needs a change in management behaviour if the destination is to be reached. Why should management change their behaviour if they have no comprehension of the need to change? Actions will always speak louder than words and nowhere is this more obvious than management actions in our typical hierarchical organisations. Management can talk quality until the cows come home (and often do) but if their actions belie their words they are doomed to failure. Too often managers launch into quality programmes with no real comprehension of the destination, let alone the vicissitudes to be met on the way.

2. Lack of vision and planning

The conversion to quality has been likened to a religious experience. There is truth in this observation. Some executives see the light and suddenly become born-again quality managers. Fired with the zeal of the new faith they go rushing off on the road to Damascus and expect everyone else to follow blindly. Unfortunately these evangelists have little real idea of where or what Damascus is, of how to get there and even less idea of what they are going to need on the journey. The conversion is total and so there is no time to be lost and certainly no time to define the purpose or vision and plan how to get there. Thomas, the sceptical executive with some questions, is berated as 'ye of little faith'. Well, good for the sceptics if they can force a pause for thought. But to continue the analogy, the path to the quality heaven demands an *organised* religion.

Incidentally, the author invariably advises his clients to include at least one sceptic in the initial planning team. In part this is because there will be many sceptics in the organisation and these issues must be faced from the start. However, experience has shown that they will raise some tough questions which can sensibly temper those of blind faith. Almost without exception, the power of the concept and of teamwork triumphs and the erstwhile sceptic becomes a powerful agent for change. The message to others becomes, 'Well, if Bill is so convinced, there must be something in this quality thing.'

W. Edwards Deming, the American quality guru, has always demanded constancy of purpose rather than commitment from management. The profound knowledge which lies at the heart of this statement is that management must first have a purpose to which to remain constant. The failure to provide this purpose and to provide a plan to achieve it is the real cause of disappointment in many quality initiatives.

The executive or leader of the organisation has to have a very clear idea of Damascus and then communicate it very clearly to all the would-be pilgrims. Many executives define fairly clearly the business objectives of the organisation but give only moderate attention to the principles and values or methods by which they want the business vision achieved. Too often that is delegated to the Human Resources or Personnel Director or in the case of quality to a 'quality team'. The resultant process has been succinctly described by Dr Stephen Tanner of The Prudential Assurance Company as 'guru-hopping'. Defining the total vision and planning constancy are major elements of Part Three of this book.

3. Satisfaction with the quick fix

Today most executives realise that quality of service is important to their customers. Naturally they want to *do* something to improve quality within their own organisation. However, few comprehend that the lack of quality that they detect in their own company could be the result of their own behaviour or actions. They are also imbued with the Western philosophy that if they turn their attention to the problem it can be quickly fixed. Consequently, the laudable desire to improve customer satisfaction and the image of the organisation is often crudely translated into another urge 'to beat up on the workers'. The language actually used is more likely to be 'motivating the workforce' or 'providing our people with a customer orientation'.

The three most common examples of the 'quick fix' mentality in attempting to improve quality in Western service organisations are:

- The introduction of quality circles.
- Customer care programmes .
- Empowering the people.

Each of these approaches is valid and indeed they can be powerful contributors to an overall process, but only if the operating environment is conducive to their success – in other words, if the executives have first created a new environment in which traditional management behaviour patterns have demonstrably changed. Without the cultural change each of the above become one-off programmes. They also delude management into believing that they have dealt with the quality issue and that they can now turn their minds to more important 'real business issues'. Even the most progressive companies can fall into the quick fix trap. Immediate application of the band-aid can hide the haemorrhaging in the body of the organisation. It is worth examining the fallacies that lie behind these approaches if applied in isolation.

Quality Circles

When the impact of the Japanese quality challenge first became apparent Western consultants and businessmen rushed to Japan. They were looking for the magic elixir that had transformed this strange nation of geisha girls and cherry blossom in a little over twenty years; changed it from being the provider of tawdry rubbish into the highest quality supplier in the world. These were expensive trips so there was little time for real research into all the issues but they did find one answer that satisfied their quick fix minds: the quality circle. For them the quality circle meant groups of workers collaborating with their supervisors to complete fishbone diagrams and solve all their quality problems. This idea appealed to Western management. It was relatively cheap to organise and it placed the responsibility for quality where they thought it belonged – with the workers. So the quality circle quickly became the latest import from Japan.

Some years later puzzled executives found it hard to explain the relative failure of the quality circle movement in the West. In the end they sighed and put it down to the difference in attitude between the Japanese and the Western worker. In one sense they were right but it never occurred to them that the difference in attitude in the workers was caused by the difference in behaviour of the respective managements. The Japanese manager understood statistical theory. They *knew* that the workers on their own could only eliminate some twenty per cent of the sources of error. They had to participate actively with the workers in tackling the remaining eighty per cent. In the West, quality circles opened with enthusiasm. Contrary to much management belief, workers would like to take pride in their jobs and eliminate the hassle of continuous defects. But enthusiasm waned when every one of the 'eighty per cent problems' was greeted by management with a dismissive 'good idea but get on with your work'.

The reader should not infer from this that the author is against the concept of quality circles. In fact he is an enthusiastic supporter, though in practice he talks of improvement groups and innovation groups to escape the name association. However, in the author's experience, quality circles are doomed to comparative failure if management do not wholly understand their personal role in the process.

Customer Care

Customer care programmes are the most prevalent of the quick fix approaches to quality improvement in service organisations. Providing pleasant waiting rooms, teaching staff to treat the customer with courtesy and how to handle the telephone are important ingredients in giving a quality service. However, used in isolation it will generally only gloss over the cracks in providing a real quality service. Some examples make the point.

A frequent traveller was waiting to check in at the airline desk. The passenger in front was screaming abuse at the attendant, telling her what he thought of her incompetent airline. Throughout the tirade she smiled sweetly and dealt with him with the utmost courtesy. Eventually the passenger moved on, still muttering about awful service. Our curious frequent traveller moved up to the desk, handed over his tickets and asked the attendant, 'I was very impressed with the way that you handled that irate passenger; tell me, have you been on a customer care programme?' Still with a sweet smile she replied, 'No sir, it is the power of knowledge.' A little puzzled, the traveller repeated, 'The power of knowledge?' And oh so sweetly she said, 'Yes sir, you see both he and I know that he is flying to Miami but only I know that his baggage is going to Chicago.'

All of us have met the smiling hotel receptionist who provides a tinge of delight at the beginning of our stay. But this is little consolation when room service takes an hour to deliver a tepid pot of coffee and a wrinkled sandwich, or there are no towels in the bathroom. Similarly, the courteous cashier at the bank does not compensate for the missed automatic payment or the incorrectly returned cheque. All the care in the world from the front office or those having direct contact with the customer is of little avail if the back office does not perform.

Customer care can be an easy way out for service industries. It stems from the obvious fact that they are primarily people businesses. Their management contrast their operations with the machine-dominated systemised production lines of manufacturing and consider that there is no correlation. They fail to recognise that they also deliver service through a series of systemised processes which require many similar controls and aids. They may well be applied differently but they are similar in concept. Service organisations must ensure that all the back office processes are right *and* train the front office to care for the customer. Actually, if all the behind-the-scenes processes are in control, the people with direct customer contact will be smiling naturally. They will be happy in their work because they have no irate customers to calm down.

Empowering the People

Empowering the people is a more complex issue. It depends on what the organisation means by empowering. The full meaning of the phrase goes to the very heart of TCI and the author's central philosophy. However, like other quality concepts it is in danger of being prostituted. It is very much in vogue with consultants in the USA and is gaining ground in the UK. In many cases it is a short fix extension of customer care, giving the direct customer contact more latitude in providing extras to delight the customer. Allowing the counterhand at a burger bar to provide the customer with as many sachets of ketchup as he desires rather than the previous standard of just the one is merely amending the tolerance on the standard. To allow the same counterhand to refuse to serve a whole batch of burgers because they did not come up to standard could be viewed as empowering the people. Similarly, in the manufacturing industries the production line was once sacrosanct and only a very senior individual, probably only the plant manager himself, was authorised to stop the line. Now in some plants the operator can close down the line if he spots a defect. That is empowering the people. That is defining a standard where error is unacceptable.

The Packaged Solution

A different variant of the quick fix approach can also be seen in the service organisation that is determined to implement every element of TQM. They have recognised the need to change and naturally do not want to waste too much time in implementing a quality ethos. They are also wise enough to comprehend that they are going to need outside help and therefore they approach TQM consultants. At this stage they can easily fall prey to the complete 'packaged' methodology and a complete 'packaged' educational system.

It is difficult to criticise the executive who decides to follow this prescribed route. Many of these packaged solutions are directly, or by inference, linked to the teachings of one or other of the quality gurus. Yet, despite the undoubted credibility of the guru, these packaged solutions will ignore the unique culture of the organisation and create barriers to communication throughout the workforce.

Apart from the issue of communicating across cultures there is a tendency for this approach to be limited to training alone. In that sense the executive decision has unwittingly fallen for a quick fix solution.

4. The process became tool-bound

A substantial armoury of tools has been developed over the years to support all involved in the quality improvement process. A number are described in Chapter 23. They range from relatively simple measurement and process analysis tools, through a series of problem-solving techniques, to very sophisticated use of statistical concepts. Many of these tools and techniques will actually assist the mindset change and are therefore an integral part of the improvement strategy. Others have their use in specific situations.

However, TCI will not be achieved by tools alone. Some organisations become so obsessed with the tools themselves that they forget that tools are there only for a purpose. Trying to measure every element of a process from the outset will drown the organisation with facts that it cannot use or take action on. When measurement charts are being used as an alternative to wallpaper it is a reasonable bet that nothing much will change. Some people spend so much time filling in charts and collecting statistics that there is little time left to complete their real work.

Many proponents of Statistical Process Control (SPC) seem to believe that the use of this undoubtedly powerful tool is all that is needed to achieve TCI. Of course SPC contains a range of measurement tools which need careful selection to meet given circumstances. They are all designed to assist in the control of work processes, which is the central core of continuous improvement. Nevertheless, *control* is not the only factor in looking at or managing the human element of work.

Dr Tanner, mentioned previously, describes an experience which aptly sums up the tool-bound trap. He then worked for a major car manufacturer which was, ostensibly, very committed to SPC. The UK plants were being continually admonished on the efficiency of their colleagues in the Continental European plants and one example cited by management was their use of SPC. So on a visit to their Belgian plant he naturally looked for evidence of this vaunted use of SPC to take back to the UK. To his surprise, as he was shown around the plant, he noted that many of the SPC control charts indicated that the processes being measured were 'out of control'. He questioned the Quality Control Superintendent, who quickly agreed with him that this was the case, but added that it didn't really matter. The important thing was that the charts were displayed line-side so that senior management thought that the production unit were doing a good job. The production and quality management were gambling, correctly, that senior management could not understand SPC so all they were looking for was evidence that charts were being displayed and filled in. Dr Deming may wail that management is inadequately trained and does not understand statistics but to insist on a tool-bound route will only perpetuate the senseless fog.

Similarly, national quality systems such as BS 5750 and ISO 9000 are useful disciplines but by themselves will not ensure quality of service. Too many organisations go through the task of certification to such systems for marketing reasons alone: in other words, as suppliers to other organisations they need such certification to remain in business. They will improve but unless they see the wider ramifications of quality they will not achieve what they might have expected. These systems can become another form of management cop-out: 'Good, now we have been certified we have dealt with quality.'

Service industries, prompted by marketing considerations, are showing a healthy interest in BS 5750, which can assist their quality revolution. However, this interest can also lead them into a dangerous cul-de-sac closely related to allowing quality to become institutionalised. Meeting the requirements for certification appears complicated and technical to service management. There is a resulting tendency to delegate the whole process to the quality departments. Up to a point that is reasonable but the inherent risk is that the quality department will then be seen as the key change agents for TCI. That is a disastrous viewpoint. Quality has become too constraining.

5. Quality too constraining

The concepts promoted in this book seek to address the *whole* way in which work is organised. This is why the words 'culture change' appear so often. In that context quality is an umbrella which covers a whole host of managerial theory. Without that understanding the very word quality can be too constraining.

The word quality can be an impediment to even getting started. Too few executives see quality as a strategic imperative. They are more likely to see it as a task to be delegated to a quality department and in any case as an expense item to be controlled. They rarely see it as permeating everything that happens in the organisation. When quality does find a place on their agenda and they want to take action they are likely to adopt the quick fix route.

Competition has led many organisations to elevate quality to the strategic level. But here again the word 'quality' imposes constraints. They may agree with Philip Crosby that quality should be equal to revenue, cost and schedule but still see each of those elements as separate functions or fortresses. In some ways this attitude is the more disappointing. Having seen the light, it is then dissipated. Tremendous energy is thrown into the quality improvement process and everyone in the organisation is enthused but there is no real and lasting change. This level of comprehension will often lead to quality improvement becoming institutionalised into a self-perpetuating bureaucracy.

The need to improve is first recognised through the competitive market need to provide quality services. That need will not be wholly met if quality is constrained by lack of comprehension of what is now meant by that word. Quality should be viewed as the outcome rather than the process.

6. Culture change versus project approach

The gurus and writers on the subject of quality improvement naturally each have their own emphasis on how best to approach implementation. It would be unwise to select anyone to be either wholly
right or wholly wrong. In as much as it is possible they should be
viewed in their totality. However, the author detects a disturbing
trend in organisations embarking on quality improvement and
within the consultancies advising them.

Increasingly the overall philosophy of quality management is
being artificially divided into two distinct and competing implementation strategies. The two approaches are categorised as the 'overall
culture change route' and the 'project by project approach'. This
dangerous dichotomy is being fostered largely by consultants
striving to find their own unique selling point. Some of them even
quote or misinterpret other gurus (without their consent) to support
their distinct methodology or package. The proponents of either, as
competing rather than as integral implementation philosophies, are
leading their clients into very dangerous waters.

The culture change route is sometimes castigated by its oppo-
nents as 'motherhood'. Certainly if misapplied it will produce little
real improvement in quality or productivity. The concept is based
largely on cascading education and training for everyone in the
organisation. This process is designed to lead everyone to recognise
the need to change and provide them with the competence to
analyse and improve work processes. There is nothing wrong in this
approach – indeed it is an essential element in quality improvement.
The danger lies in the organisational tendency for everyone to wait
until the educational process is complete before tackling the major
problems discovered on the way. By then they will have forgotten
much that was learnt. This is a particular danger for middle management. At its worst it can be likened to insisting that everyone stays
on the fire prevention course while the east wing burns down.

The opposing 'project by project' approach is more pragmatic and
is argued to be more practical. The fashionable 'business process re-
engineering' (BPR) exhibits some of these tendencies. In essence a
series of key issues, processes or opportunities for improvement are
identified and then task forces or project teams are established to
work on the issues. Of course, each team is educated and trained in
techniques to accomplish their allotted task. To some extent a culture
change does take place by the very nature of the activity. The danger
is that the education, training and experience is not common and
many functions such as clerical and secretarial are not wholly

involved. There is also a tendency to create a large supporting quality organisation of full-time trainers and facilitators. In the broadest sense the new way of working does not enter the overall fabric of the organisation.

The real answer lies in the scope of the original assessment and planning stage of the TCI process. The assessment will highlight both the culture change required and the immediate key success factors. The plan should then address an implementation strategy that ensures that both approaches are integral rather than competing. It will avoid the dangers inherent in each when taken as the sole route. Perhaps the integrated approach becomes more akin to parenthood rather than mere motherhood!

7. Quality management became institutionalised

Using TQM as a process to achieve TCI does require some initial facilitative organisation to plan and support the process of change. However, that organisation should never be seen as responsible for quality; that is the responsibility of the normal structure of management and people working together. To emphasise that important concept the initial TQM organisation should plan the timing of its own extinction right from the outset.

Unfortunately, in many organisations fully committed to quality improvement a proliferation of quality improvement teams, facilitators and coordinators establish a permanent ownership of quality. Another fortress has been created and the normal structure of the organisation is soon throwing its quality problems over the wall to the 'quality people'.

This abiding sin of quality initiatives usually stems from a generalised and packaged methodology. Large sums of money are spent on this generic education or methodology and then even larger sums are expended over long periods of time on a semi-permanent TQM bureaucracy. This tendency is very prevalent in large companies or public organisations. Their culture inherently encourages empire-building (or at least until the next pruning exercise) and they have a natural tendency to purchase what they are led to believe are 'tried and proven methodologies'.

To provide some perspective to these assertions the author contends that an organisation of, say, 2,000 employees should not require more than two full-time employees with secretarial assistance to manage a TQM process. In the first year to eighteen months they will need the part-time secondment of facilitators and internal instructors but at the end of that period quality improvement should be the natural responsibility of managers and employees doing their normal jobs. The only factor that might extend that permanent resource is locational dispersion. It should be added that this yardstick should not be automatically applied to any existing quality function staff. They have a distinct function of metrology rather than company-wide quality improvement: one might argue that traditional quality managers should be retitled measurement managers to avoid the traditional misconception.

8. The people were not really involved

This reason for failure is really the result of other causal factors rather than a root cause in its own right. However, it is so often quoted as a cause of failure that it deserves separate consideration. Typical statements of companies experiencing this issue are as follows:

- 'Nothing really changed.'
- 'The shop floor didn't actually do anything.'
- 'Somehow it didn't really happen.'
- 'Though initially greeted with enthusiasm, the workers never "bought in"'.
- 'Deep down the workers were not interested.'

Earlier in this book the issue was raised of why the manager should change his behaviour. The answer was that unless he does, the attitude of the worker will not change – and we might add, 'why should it?' Primarily this is an issue of recognition of the need to change depending on our role in the organisation. We all need to change but we will all have different motivations. Once again, the responsibility falls on management. When they understand that their principal role is to help their people we are nearer the solution. Chapter 19 examines the issue of involving the people in more depth.

9. Lack of real business measurables

A central tenet of TCI can be summed up in the phrase 'what you cannot measure, you cannot manage', to which could be added 'what you do not measure, you are probably not managing'. Yet all too many total quality management processes are not measured in a meaningful way. Some companies mistakenly believe they are measuring the process by techniques such as the Cost of Quality but few apply real business measurables as the criteria for success.

Cost of Quality reigned supreme for over a decade as the real measure of the quality process. This was largely due to the teaching of Philip Crosby, who defined it as one of the four absolutes of quality improvement. COQ can be a powerful tool to identify need and to establish priorities for corrective action but it has demonstrable weaknesses when used as an overall measure of the whole process. In the opinion of the author, its practical application as the total measure has the following weaknesses:

• The regular measurement of COQ done properly across the whole organisation is a costly diversion of resource. Interestingly, it is akin to inspection and its cost could be added to the original estimate of wasted resource.
• As the comprehension of what really constitutes a nonconformance grows so does the perceived value of COQ. In other words, the original measure goes up rather than down over the first year.
• Non-conformances are often caused in another operative department than those in which they are found, and opportunities for improvement differ across the organisation. The COQ process is often incorrectly used as a measure of departmental performance which can be grossly unjust and thus set up resistance to the whole quality process.
• In real operational practice managers who control budgets can manipulate COQ estimates to appear to be what they want them to be.

It is of interest that one of the successful pioneers in quality management (3M) who originally used COQ as the overall measure decided to stop using it a few years ago.

The original reason most companies invest in quality management is the competitive need to improve the quality of their products and services. At that stage COQ is a powerful tool to help their understanding that they will not achieve their aims by just increasing inspection or merely motivating their workforce. But the original deficiencies that must be improved are still present and should therefore be the basis for measuring improvement. For example, if the initial assessment stage in an insurance company shows that the turnaround time from proposal to issue of a completed policy is twenty days and the competitive need is to reduce this to five days then that is the measure. Milestones can be set for a staged reduction from twenty to five days over a given time frame. Achieving those milestones would be a real business measurable. Every organisation can establish a number of such criteria which can be used as the real measure of success.

There will be arguments within the organisation about whether all these improvements are wholly the result of the quality management process. Actually, the same could be said of COQ, but what does it really matter if the focused measurables are all being achieved? However, in addition to the business measurables (which should be defined in the original plan) there are additional measures which can be established to assist those managing the TQM process. TQM should be viewed as a business process in its own right. In other words, it will have inputs and outputs which should be related to requirements. These can be used as measures by those directly involved in managing the process of change. These measures will support progress or otherwise for the executives measuring the business parameters.

PART TWO

But we are different...

Some unique aspects of service

6. WE CAN DO IT OUR WAY

Part One of this book described those principles in the management of quality that apply to both manufacturing and service organisations. It noted in passing that since manufacturing industries had proved these principles in their own administrative and service functions they also applied to the service sector. Up to a point this is true. It would therefore appear that the oft repeated cry of service organisations 'that we are different' is a false premise and had been debunked, but that would be a simplistic assumption.

Service organisations *are* different: the successful implementation of the TQM process requires that the differences are fully understood. Some differences are generic to the whole service field and others are specific to certain sectors of the service arena. This chapter addresses the generic factors and the other chapters in Part Two will examine particular sectors.

First let's be clear about some of the terminology that is used when applying quality to service. Product quality and service quality are the same in as much as they apply to the results of different activities. There are, however, some fundamental differences in the organisation of an operation to provide products and services. There are also intrinsic differences between products and services which we will examine. Customer service in this context is not the same as service quality. The former is more accurately applied to the post-delivery of a product as part of a manufacturing process.

Defective products can be put right or serviced. Most services have already been consumed or completed and cannot therefore be put right. A motor car with a defective part can be 'serviced' so that it can continue to provide 'quality'. Time lost on a late train or plane cannot be replaced.

Let's look at some of the intrinsic differences between products and services:

PRODUCT	SERVICE
• The customer receives a tangible product in the form of goods which can be seen and touched.	• The customer receives an intangible service which may or may not satisfy.
• The goods remain with the customer.	• Services are consumed at the moment of delivery.
• The production and delivery of goods are usually separated.	• Production, delivery and consumption of services are often at the same time.
• Few producers deal with customers.	• Most producers deal with customers.
• The customer is rarely involved with production.	• The customer is often closely involved with production.
• Goods can be serviced	• Services have already been consumed and cannot be serviced.
• Goods are subject to liability but the producer has more opportunity to ameliorate the effect on the customer and thus the financial penalty.	• Services which do not meet the requirements are difficult to replace – the financial impact is usually total.
• Goods can be purchased to store in inventory to satisfy the customer's needs.	• Services cannot be stored but must still be available on customer demand.
• Goods can be transported to the point of sale.	• Some services are transportable (e.g. information through communication lines) but most require the transportation of the service provider.
• The quality of goods is relatively easy for customers to evaluate.	• The quality of services is more dependent on subjective perception and expectation.
• Goods are often technically complex – the customer therefore feels more reliant on the producer.	• Services appear less complex – the customer therefore feels qualified to hassle the producer.

The differences highlighted in this list should be enough to demonstrate that service organisations have every right to claim that they are different. But there is another lesson to be learnt from these differences. The customer of both product and service is now much more aware of quality and has higher expectations than in the past. These expectations are steadily being satisfied and heightened by the manufacturers. The spotlight has now turned onto the service sector. The evidence from the list of contrasts indicates that it may be more difficult for the service provider to meet those rising expectations – if only for the reason that the service provider usually has only one chance to delight the customer. The imperative to change is therefore the greater.

Organisationally there are more differences that must be taken into account in planning the introduction of TQM. Those already listed are primarily based on an external perspective. Consider the internal contrasts between manufacturing and service.

MANUFACTURING	SERVICE
• Production is capital or equipment orientated.	• Production is people orientated.
• Technical skills dominate.	• Inter-personal skills dominate.
• Training will dominate.	• Education will dominate.
• Production results are variable.	• Production results are more variable.

The list could be extended but the point is obvious: the executives in manufacturing and service organisations do face different issues. For one thing all these differences create different perceptions in the minds of the customer and the employee. The people-dominated service sector will have a tendency to harbour more knowledge workers such as consultants and actuaries who believe that they work on their own and are independent of the organisation. These 'prima donnas' lead to remote layers in the organisation and exaggerate the division between the thinkers and the doers. There is a tendency in the service organisation for the point of contact with the customer to be with the lowest-paid employees of the organisation. The decision-makers become remote from the market place and are slow to react to changing customer perceptions. The traditional and outdated control, command and compliance approach to management dominates.

However, it would be wrong to assume that service organisations do not produce products from work processes. Many service companies can be categorised as 'paper factories'. They produce packages of information on paper, such as:

Designs	Manuals	Policies	Presentations
Reports	Contracts	Diagnoses	Specifications
Consultations	Proposals	Schedules	Training courses

One area which causes considerable difficulty in the service sector is the confusion that exists between 'process' quality and 'outcome' quality. Outcome quality is often wholly dependent on the specialists or consultants – the ability of the actuary or the surgeon. Calls for quality improvement therefore meet resistance from the specialist who can interpret the initiative as an attack on their professional integrity. Irrespective of whether their performance or outcome should be measured, they find it difficult to understand that they do not stand alone but are dependent on supporting processes. Most certainly their client or patient will be evaluating the process quality as part of their whole experience. Look at the division of these two aspects of quality for a patient entering hospital for surgery:

Process quality
- Admissions and ward staff friendly, responsive and professional.
- Ward quiet, clean and well equipped with patient-oriented service as well as technical equipment.
- Food good and sufficient.
- Visitor relations handled well.

Outcome quality
- Patient recovers.
- Limited after-effects.
- Wounds heal quickly.

This example typifies the rapidly evolving focus on the public sector as a major element in the quality revolution. The trend is not confined to the UK, but the general election campaign in Britain in 1992 emphasised this aspect. All three main political parties in one way or another have elevated service to the consumer (i.e. the electorate) to a high level of priority. The quality of the National Health Service and of public education dominated the electioneering.

Politicians have a tendency to react to the prevailing opinion or mood of their electorates rather than stride out in advance of public opinion. So the focus on the public sector is in reality customer-driven and it is therefore unlikely to go away. Indeed, the Conservative Party has now introduced a broad Citizens' Charter with a host of sector-specific charters almost totally directed at the public sector. These charters, with their performance criteria and non-performance penalties, are supported by legislation. In other words, the legislature has decided to support the consumer against the executive (civil servants or quasi-government employees) in the provision of quality services. Historically these public service sectors such as health, education, public transportation, the Post Office, public utilities, Social Security and the Inland Revenue have been protected from this level of customer scrutiny. There was a time when citizens dutifully paid their taxes and were resigned to accept what government provided. They were probably thankful that they did not get all the government they had paid for! Those days appear to be over. The public service sector will have to respond.

It was stated earlier that goods are tangible – they can be touched by the customer – while services are intangible. This makes the measurement of customer expectations more difficult for the service provider. It is true that customers are now influenced by the intangible services that surround a manufactured product. Nevertheless, the spectrum of customer expectation is wider and more complex in most service situations.

What are the variables that differentiate one service provider from another? Take airlines for example. The aircraft are not much different; indeed most of them are manufactured by the same company. The same applies to the seats and the airline has little control over the airport it uses. Even prices are broadly similar. Yet most frequent travellers can quickly name their own favourite airline. The decision is based on the intangibles of service, usually related to human rather than technical values.

Recently the author was asked to name his favourite airlines and without hesitation replied Virgin and Emirates. He was then asked to name an internal American airline. Though his recent experience was limited, he replied Delta. The next week he began a month-long speaking tour of the USA. As luck would have it the first internal flight was with Delta: but it was a disaster. First the plane was nearly an hour late in departing. This was caused by a protracted argument inside the aircraft about who had valid tickets. Delta had over-booked and were finding it difficult to bribe any Sunday night passengers to delay their journey until the next morning. On arrival late on Sunday night in New York there were more problems. The author flies first class and pays the extra for more room, less waiting at either end and because the baggage is first up the ramp. On this first-class Delta flight one piece of baggage did come up first as expected but the second piece was actually last up the service ramp. The author was not pleased with Delta, yet the cabin staff were all well-trained, pleasant and helpful and no doubt the pilot was excellent at his job.

What was really going wrong at Delta became obvious outside the airport. There was a huge billboard advertising Delta: the copywriter's slogan read 'We love flying...and it shows'. It certainly did; both the flight and the billboard demonstrated that Delta had forgotten the purpose of their business. The purpose of an airline is not to fly planes but to *move people* by air. They should forget about their lovely planes (up to a point – the traveller would like them well maintained) and concentrate on their lovely passengers.

Passengers judge airlines by how they are treated from the moment they purchase a ticket to the moment they collect their baggage and leave the airline's care. No amount of marketing expense or television advertising can eradicate the effect of poor frontline service. The same is true of every service operation.

The service business is primarily a people business. Too few service organisations create a sense of purpose or excitement amongst their employees. Customer satisfaction from a people business actually starts with satisfied employees, employees who find joy in their work. We will look at this in more detail in Part Three (Making it Happen).

This chapter has shown that there is a real need for quality improvement in the service sector. It has also demonstrated that there are substantial differences between manufacturing and services. The service organisations will therefore have to implement TQM in their own unique way. The following chapters look at progress and opportunities in specific service areas.

7. FINANCIAL SERVICES

'Service should run through an organisation like blood through a body.'
Dr Stephen Tanner, The Prudential Assurance Company Ltd.

The financial services industry has experienced tremendous growth and undergone great change in recent decades. In the developed countries it now employs far more people than the total for the manufacturing industries. Varying forms of deregulation, competition and more demanding customers have created an environment significantly different from that which existed only a few years ago.

The modern state cannot survive without the financial services industry. The market-driven, consumer-oriented and relatively affluent societies require a host of sophisticated financial services. The lack of such a readily available infrastructure is the greatest impediment to the orderly and rapid transition from communism to capitalism now facing Eastern Europe and the states of the former Soviet Union.

The industry, as a collective term, covers a myriad of discrete services used at one time or another by almost every individual in the land. They include routine financial transactions, provision of long-term loans for capital investment and home ownership, immediate consumer credit, insurance, investment and savings, provision of pensions and healthcare and equity transactions. These services were once provided by distinct sectors of the industry such as banking, insurance, building societies, savings and loans, credit card companies and brokers. Those distinctions are now becoming steadily blurred.

The deregulation of financial services and consequent ready access to funds have produced a new competitive environment in the industry. Once distinct sectors have now moved into each others' arena. The retail banks were particularly vulnerable to such attack. They had become monolithic organisations with little recognition of the changing perceptions of their customers. They showed even less understanding of a totally new potential customer base from an upwardly rising and aspiring society. Now banks are competing with building societies in the UK, thrifts in the USA, insurance companies and stock brokers, and insurance companies and banks have competed for chains of estate agents. This new competition has brought about success for some and spectacular failure for others. Many have strayed beyond their competence to manage – as for example the Prudential Assurance fiasco with estate agencies. Rationalisation and the cold wind of recession have provided a steadying influence but the financial services industry will never be the same again. Each sector is now competing on a much wider base.

During the same period the industry has invested heavily in computers, specialist software and other forms of automation. This massive investment in automated systems (together with rationalisation) has halted the rapid rise in employment and may even lead to substantial reductions in the number of people employed in the industry. However, there is little sign that this investment has provided any sustained competitive advantage for any sector. The industry will remain the major employer and continue to be characterised as the 'people and paper' industry. To date, with some exceptions, the industry has failed to match its investment in automation with the real release of the potential of all the people it employs.

Of course the financial services industry has not been immune from or ignored the quality revolution. Initially competitive advantage was sought by new products, new pricing strategies or by automated technology. Step by step each new initiative was rapidly matched by a competitor. Customers had increasing difficulty in differentiating the offerings of individual companies but eventually financial institutions came to realise that the best way to differentiate themselves from the competition was by personal customer service.

There is an interesting paradox in this evolving relationship with customers. This book has touched upon the changing perceptions of customers and the failure of industry to recognise the change – in other words, the view that customers have changed but that the banks and other financial institutions have not changed in their approach to customers. On the surface this is true but the paradox is that deep down it is totally untrue. Customers now perceive that they have the *power* to demand service. Customers have always wanted good old-fashioned service and so, in that sense, they have not changed. The service industries are selling promises; all the customer wants is that the promises be kept. The customers' perception is that once upon a time professionals used to keep their promises and that service was a natural element of business. They believe that the institutions have changed, not them. The customers thought (at least for a few years) that this was inevitable because the world had become more complex or because of computers, so they accepted the change. The changing perception of customers is that they will *no longer accept* that they cannot have what in their view used to be the norm.

The senior management of the financial service companies made the decision to improve their services to customers to provide the competitive differential. Apart from commissioned customer surveys it is interesting to consider their own level of customer contact as a factor in their decisions and as to how they were to be implemented.

Customer complaints are an obvious source of customer concerns. John Goodman, President of strategic consultants TARP Europe Ltd, presented to a conference in March 1991 his company's research into this area. He referred to it as the 'Tip of the Iceberg Phenomenon' (see Figure 5). The key fact illustrated is that at least 50 per cent of customers who encounter problems just do not complain. Of the others, 45 per cent complain only to a front-line retail employee who will either handle or mishandle the complaint. Very few of those complaints will be recorded and noted to management. Only 5 per cent will complain to senior management, and even these are often just delegated back to the front-line employees. TARP has found several instances of ratios as high as 2,000 problem occurrences to one report to the corporate level. Management is

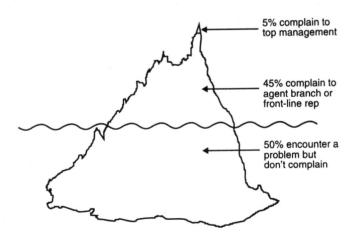

Figure 5. The tip of the iceberg phenomenon

concentrating its attention on the significant few issues and do not even know about the thousands of insignificant many issues which in reality are forming customer perceptions of the company.

Customer complaints should always be seen as an opportunity to eliminate error and establish customer views but they are themselves reactive opportunities to special events. The real opportunities for the continuous sounding of customer views and understanding of their needs come from the regular contact with customers during business transactions.

Figure 6 demonstrates a dramatic lesson for the management of financial service companies. In terms of numbers of transactions (not the financial value of the transactions) the executives and senior operational management have regular contact with only 3 per cent of their customers. Only 5 per cent of transactions involve lower-level management (e.g. bank managers), but perhaps the most dramatic of all the sections of the pie chart is the indication that some 65 per cent of transactions involve no individual contact with employees of the organisation. There is a limit to the 'user-friendliness' that can be built into an automatic teller machine. However, at some stage or another the majority of customers will make direct contact with the 'front line' or lowest-paid members of the organisation.

Figure 6. Level of customer contact for regular transactions

When faced with these kind of facts and their obvious interest in satisfying customers, one would naturally expect the executives and senior operational management to eagerly seek the opinions of the lowest-level customer contacts: it is an interesting supposition but far removed from reality. Western management has a long way to go before it really understands the Japanese concept of 'going to *gemba'*, or the workplace. Senior management is caught in the mindset of the division between the 'thinkers' and the 'doers' (which will be examined in Part Three of this book). They fail to recognise that the person actually doing the job – in other words, in contact with the customer – might actually know what is happening.

Until the competitive eighties the giants of the financial services industry, such as the banks and the major insurance companies, had a relatively static customer base. Customers rarely changed banks or their insurance agents. The giants slumbered and concentrated on internal issues and ran the organisation to suit themselves or their staff. They closed on Saturdays, jobs were secure and promotional prospects were handled by piling deputy assistant general managers upon assistant general managers and so on throughout the organisation. Communication and response to the customer became slower and slower. Then suddenly the world changed; there were new hungry and customer-aware wolves roaming the High Street. Banks had to re-open on Saturdays, stop adding bank charges to accounts in credit and, horror of horrors, even pay interest on current accounts in credit. Competition began to wake up the leviathans. Service and customer care became a strategic issue.

The whole tenor of bank (and other financial institutions') promotion and advertising demonstrated a volte-face by bank management. The enduring theme of security epitomised by stone façades and wood-panelled offices for bank managers changed almost overnight. Now there were 'listening banks' and 'caring banks' and 'the girl at the Woolwich'. They had realised that customers were choosing their financial institutions on the basis of personal service encounters. The change was almost too sudden. The cynical press and customers delighted in stories about banks who had not 'listened' or 'cared'. Then, as recession began to bite, exposed banks ran into other problems. The National Westminster in particular took a terrible caning on its perceived treatment of small businesses, which it had previously encouraged. To be objective, some of the criticism was unfounded but the banks had been hoisted on a classic petard. Their new-style promotion had established benchmarks or expectations which their organisations and cultures were not yet in a position to meet. The tellers and cashiers were now all smiling and greeting the customer by name. The bank managers were also smiling (even listening) and placing the customer in a soft armchair with a cup of coffee. But none of them had really been empowered to change anything substantial.

The major institutions had realised the new power of the customer. As a result they launched a series of 'customer care programmes' which included staff training, an attempt to remove error, complete remodelling of many customer contact branches and a determined attack on 'customer queueing' issues. Some, mostly in the USA, went as far as to establish service guarantees with recompense to the customer if the guarantee was not met. For example, the Chemical Bank presented customers with a $5 note if they had waited more than seven minutes. They did invest in market research and constructively listen to complaints. They encouraged their branch staff to make suggestions as to how to improve service to customers. The banks, building societies and insurance companies invested heavily in customer care and their whole image. In the main there was a positive return on the investment; they did *substantially* improve their day-to-day service and attitude to the customer. Redressing the balance, it is only fair to point out that the National Westminster Bank 'Quality Service Programme' probably went further and achieved more than their main competitors in the area of customer care. Paul Goodstadt, head of the quality service department at the National Westminster Bank, has stated that the bank 'believes that it is only as good as the last transaction. Customers have short memories, but bad service experiences cannot be erased from their minds.'

Financial institutions have made substantial progress in improving customer service and customer care. There is also tremendous interest in TQM but there does seem to be a wide variance in what individual organisations believe that TQM really means. With some notable exceptions most initiatives under the quality banner seem to confuse quality with customer care. Quality does not seem to have permeated the whole organisation as a way of life. Concentrating on the front end of the organisation is equivalent to asking ten per cent of the people to concentrate on solving customer problems while ninety per cent of the people are busily creating new problems. Though there are exceptions, in general quality initiatives in the financial service companies in Europe and the USA fall short of the greater objective on the following counts:

- Most lack an executive-driven service improvement vision or *strategy*.
- The initiatives are delegated to lower levels and rarely involve senior management.

- Organisational and internal business objectives take precedence over customer needs.
- Most are short-term programmes rather than an on-going process of improvement.
- Quality is not seen as an integral part of overall business improvement.

There are exceptions to the general rule. Several companies in the financial sector do provide evidence of a greater and deeper commitment to continuous improvement. Contrary to general opinion the author has seen little evidence of more advanced thinking in the USA. Most are still wholly absorbed in the area of customer care but one insurance company in the USA is worthy of mention. The State Farm Insurance Company in the USA has had a customer-driven

Within the insurance industry, success is typically measured in millions and billions. But in the marketplace, success is measured by a far different yardstick. Policyholders form their judgment based on how they are served in a one-to-one situation.

Our millions of policies were sold one at a time. Our claims are settled in the same way.

The whole Good Neighbour idea is based on this philosophy. State Farm strives to be the best insurance company, not necessarily the largest. Being the best requires agents and employees who are caring and courteous toward our customers. It requires sound management. It requires people who know their jobs.

Edward B. Rust, President
1958-1985

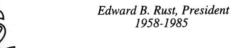

Figure 7. Statement from the State Farm Insurance Company

philosophy since their establishment in 1972 and the TQM approach has been a natural management evolvement. The statement of Edward Rust, their President until 1985 (see Figure 7), is an example of their approach.

In Germany the banks have always had a strong emphasis on transactional or process management and that probably has made a major contribution to their success. In France, Crédit Lyonnais is an example of commitment to an overall process of continuous improvement. In the UK, Girobank has transformed their operations with an organisation-wide process. Outside the banking arena financial service companies who have enhanced their reputation with their commitment to TQM include Allied Dunbar, London and Edinburgh and Save and Prosper.

One organisation in the UK has been recognised with a series of awards for its contribution to the quality revolution in the financial services industry. The Life Administration group of the Home Service Division of the Prudential Assurance Company Ltd has demonstrated the power of TQM in improved business measurables and customer satisfaction. In 1991 and 1992 this major corporation won the UK National Training Award for their quality training, the Northern Ireland Quality Award, the Institute of Administrative Management Award, and became the first insurance company to be certified to BS 5750 (ISO 9000). All of these awards required evidence of substantial improvement in such areas as productivity, speed of response, accuracy and customer satisfaction. The Prudential point the way for the financial services industry.

8. GOVERNMENT

'Every country has the government it deserves.'
Joseph de Maistre, 1811

'Be thankful that we do not get all the government we pay for.'
Attributed to Will Rodgers.

This chapter concentrates on central government though, as you will see, that very title is steadily becoming a misnomer. Later chapters will concentrate on the specific issues of healthcare, education and local government.

The eighties witnessed the first steps to halt the relentless growth of government bureaucracy, which has so epitomised this century. Around the world the whole purpose, structure and behaviour of the public services are being questioned radically. The word 'quality' has now entered the lexicon of the warring factions in the political battle over the future of the public services. Nowhere is this battle more evident than in the UK. Margaret Thatcher made 'privatisation' and 'removing the yoke of government from the people' major planks in her political philosophy. She succeeded to the extent that the whole ground for political debate in this area was fundamentally shifted. In the 1992 British General Election both right and left protagonists on the political divide paraded their own 'Citizens' Charter' and espoused the need for quality and service in the public sector.

The initial argument was summarised in a 1989 document published by the left-wing Institute of Public Policy Research in the UK by Anna Coote and Naomi Pfeiffer entitled *Is Quality Good for You?* They stated that: 'For the Right, a new-found concern for "quality" has been part of a move to re-structure public services along quasi-commercial lines and is closely connected with the idea of "value for money". For the Left, it appears to occupy a significant new position, between traditional goals. For while the Left still wants to achieve greater social and economic equality, it is now keen to distance itself from the idea that equality means uniformity; it wants a more pluralistic and responsive system, in which individuals have greater liberty to determine how their needs are met.'

Now the argument has moved on and the 'egalitarian' John Major of the Right has been stealing left-wing clothes. He has established a whole new department of state to ensure that the 'Next Step' is accomplished and has a defined requirement to establish citizens' rights to appeal against decisions, to have access to information, advice and advocacy, and protection from discrimination. These 'rights' were earlier proclaimed as part of the Left rebuttal of Margaret Thatcher's drive for efficiency. John Major could just be the first national leader to really understand the concepts of total quality.

The 'Next Step' project was devised by the Whitehall Efficiency Unit at the instigation of Prime Minister Thatcher to succeed the initial 'Privatisation Programme'. It sought to identify individual services and functions and convert those not considered suitable for full privatisation into free-standing, self-administered businesses, or executive agencies, while remaining within the government orbit. They would be ultimately responsible to the departments of state and the National Audit Commission but would be freed from many of the constraints of the normal Civil Service pattern. Hopefully, many of the new agencies would actually contribute to the public purse rather than be a never-ending drain on resources.

Government consists of a vast number of different organisations meeting diverse needs. Yet each of these is 'managed' by a uniform Civil Service culture. The 'Next Step' project was envisioned as an evolutionary process of devolving executive power which will ultimately encompass three quarters of the whole Civil Service. It has been likened to shaping the Civil Service into an organisation similar to multinational companies like Hanson, with a tight-knit strategic corporate head office. The scope of this approach can be demonstrated by the following representative list of executive agencies already formed or planned for inclusion:

• Vehicle Inspectorate	• Social Security Benefits	• Forensic Science
• Companies House	• Central Office of Information	• Property Holdings
• HM Stationery Office	• Air Officer Training	• Navy Hydrography
• National Weights and Measures	• Military Surveys	• Employment Service
• Pollution Laboratories	• Driving Tests and Training	• IB for Agriculture

- Resettlement Agency
- Civil Service College
- Conference Centres
- Historic Palaces
- Laboratory Government Chemist
- Defence Research
- Planning Inspectorate

- Driver Vehicle Licensing
- Meteorological Office
- Passport Office
- Royal Parks
- Building Research
- Veterinary Medicine

- Occupational Health
- Historic Buildings
- Patent Office
- HM Land Registry
- Insolvency Service
- Central Statistical Office

It could also be said that this list demonstrates the degree to which the all-enveloping tentacles of government bureaucracy had spread. When the major sectors that have been or are intended to be fully privatised are added to the list there can be no doubt that the change is radical. Indeed, it is a British perestroika.

None of this restructuring has been easy or without strong opposition. The political opposition to privatisation has become less vociferous but in general the debate is not over, as opposition to the educational and health service reforms indicates. The more traditional and conservative elements of the Civil Service establishment have viewed the changes with concern and alarm. Any devotee of the TV programme 'Yes, Minister' will wholly understand the power of inertia exerted by the 'mandarins' or the 'Sir Humphrey Applebys' of the Civil Service in Whitehall. Similarly, the public service trade unions are concerned at the decentralising of pay and conditions bargaining. Union leaders committed to a national negotiating machinery see a diminution of their power with the extension of 'commercial' thinking. The process of change is by no means over or certain to be achieved.

TQM has already been described as an 'agent of change'– a method of changing from a traditional managerial culture to one based on continuous improvement. In its broadest context that is exactly the change that the Civil Service is undergoing. TQM could be the ideal driving force to accomplish these new initiatives. Yet there is little evidence that it is so viewed.

To be fair, some of the new executive agencies, notably Her Majesty's Stationery Office, are implementing TQM initiatives. The Civil Service College, the educational arm for the managerial Civil Service, does provide a syllabus of quality courses but they could hardly be described as inculcating the concepts espoused in this book. The author in some of his work with the Department of Trade and Industry has considered it somewhat ironic that the government's own excellent programme to encourage industry to invest in TQM has not with the same vigour turned its focus on the very business of government itself. In reality it is a perception problem. Of all the service organisations described in this book the one most apt to declare 'that you have to understand that *we are different*' is the Civil Service.

There are of course *real* differences between the public services and private sector companies. These can be summarised as follows:

- *Profit motive:* Public service organisations are not primarily driven or motivated by bottom-line profit considerations. There are signs that some of the entrepreneurial executive agencies are becoming imbibed with that spirit but it is not a common attitude in the public services.
- *Budget process:* Funding of the public services is still primarily conducted with an emphasis on the *current financial year*. Industry suffers from some of this syndrome but not to the same extent. The author well remembers, when he headed Government Marketing for a large computer corporation, instructing his sales force to visit even the smallest establishment of the customer base during January and February to attempt to mop up the last vestiges of departmental budgets which would be lost if not spent by government year-end. The cumulative amount of small upgrades, extra discs and printers, etc., could often amount to a few million pounds' contribution to the revenue target. More sensible policies are emerging but it probably needs a major management (political) commitment to move away from the traditional annual National Budget.
- *Customer focus:* Many in the Civil Service find it difficult to determine the customer they should be delighting. For some it is the 'Minister' or current political master; for others it is the 'esprit de corps' of the service itself. Again the agencies and the whole political climate are beginning to adjust this focus to the public or consumer of the service.
- *Attitude:* The leading welfare services such as National Health and Education face real public need and tend to have the immediate reaction, when facing difficulties in meeting the demand, 'Why don't the government give us more money' – the basis for all democratic arguments about the deployment of resources.
- *Management commitment:* The traditional arm's-length communication barriers practised by the Civil Service mandarins makes it very difficult to obtain the level of on-going management commitment required for real change.

- *A major advantage:* The public sector does have a basic advantage in the quality revolution. Most government employees have a far stronger desire to 'serve' than commonly exists in the private sector. This is particularly prevalent in the caring services but it is an essential part of Civil Service culture. Even the most mundane public services have reacted naturally to 'customer care' programmes. The author has denigrated management initiatives on customer care as an example of quick-fix quality. That is true if that is all that is exhibited. Nevertheless, it is a very powerful cultural asset for the change required because it is shared at every level of public services.

Throughout the world the government service attracts a high proportion of the best trained minds produced by their respective countries' educational system. The government system then has a tendency to bond them into an élitist group out of touch with reality. Using the principles of total and continuous improvement to accelerate the change in the system of government could release a potential to the advantage of every nation.

9. RETAIL AND DISTRIBUTION

'Qualities too elevated often unfit a man for society. We don't take
ingots with us to market; we take silver or small change.'
Nicholas-Sebastian Chamfort 1794

The retail and distribution industry is the most customer-focused
sector of all industries. Nothing has changed; it always has been.
From the medieval market-place to High or Main Street and now to
the great Malls, its very survival has depended on understanding
volatile customers. More than any other industry it is dependent on
the day-to-day decisions of customers.

The changing face of the shopping market is part of the social
history of our times. Old names disappear and new names arise. Tie
Rack, Sock Shop and Body Shop are just examples of many such
changes. Great fortunes have been made and lost by recognising or
not recognising a fundamental change in the market. F.W.
Woolworth comes immediately to mind as an example of both. Tesco
correctly recognised a market and succeeded. They also continued to
research the market; saw a coming difference; changed their
approach and continued to succeed. J. Sainsbury, Wall-Mart and
W.H. Smith work so hard at listening to and understanding their
customers that they continuously improve and succeed. Gerald
Ratner understood his market only too well, but he made the
mistake of publicly deriding his customers and seemed surprised
when they turned away.

Retailing covers a wide spectrum of different businesses. All may
have a customer focus but there are many other factors that determine attitudes to quality and continuous improvement. The
merchandising of food, clothing, household and electrical goods,
books and periodicals, leisure products, and do-it-yourself all differ
and create differing management challenges. Even within these few
categories (and there are many others) there are diverse specialisations. Clothing, for example, has many facets, each marketed differently. Just consider the divisions between men's and women's

clothes, sportswear and children's clothes, off-the-peg and tailored, underwear and accessories, overcoats and leisure wear, basic and high fashion. The old traditional butcher, baker, dairy, greengrocer and fishmonger touch only a part of modern food retailing. Retail outlets and selling methods vary significantly in their managerial issues. They can vary from small kiosk to large shop or supermarket, from direct mail to the coming explosion of 'factory outlets', from department store to hypermarket. It is clear that to generalise about the retailing industry would be dangerous indeed.

However, there are two sectors which are particularly relevant to the discussion on quality. Those staples to human survival, food and clothing, exhibit characteristics which have put leaders in those areas in the forefront of the quality revolution. They may not have called their management approach 'total quality management' but the nature of their businesses intuitively led them along that path. Marks and Spencer have already been mentioned in that context but there are others such as J. Sainsbury and, though from another sector, W.H. Smith. Their management has been and generally still is based on the principles of continuous improvement. Indeed, they have not only been ahead of their manufacturing brethren but their management practices have driven their concepts into food processing and clothing manufacture. It is worthwhile considering why these companies should have shown the lead.

Each of these companies was founded by entrepreneurs with great energy and vision. But that is not the only reason, because over the same period other entrepreneurs with marketing vision have soared across the sky but eventually crashed to earth. Their sustained competitive advantage has been achieved by adherence to a vision but one that is much wider and deeper than that of seeing a market opportunity. They certainly understood their chosen markets but also established a culture that continuously monitored those markets (or listened to their customers) so that they were in a position to lead as customer perceptions changed. But above all they understood the constraints of their businesses and the role of people and processes in the organisation of their companies. The vision of these company founders created highly successful cultures which were well communicated to successive generations of managers and workers. It is not an accident that each of these companies invests well above the norm in the development of their people.

It is also not an accident that both Marks and Spencer and J. Sainsbury have been successful in markets other than their original focus, although only in the case of markets that exhibited similar characteristics: stray from their managerial culture and they face difficulties. J. Sainsbury has moved successfully from food into the do-it-yourself market with their Homebase operations. Marks and Spencer moved successfully from clothing to food but appear unable to develop the same success in the furniture and tailoring market. Both companies are famed for their quality and value for money. They have had little time for the 'quick-fix' promotion of their businesses through gimmicks or Green Shield stamps.

The characteristics of the food and general clothing businesses are relatively similar. The obvious similarity is that whatever happens people will always want food and clothes, but it would be unwise to base a successful business on that premise alone. Tastes in specific foods and fashions in clothes are constantly changing. This fact demands a high management focus on the customer and detailed knowledge of perceptible changes in selling patterns *as they happen*. The real similarity that has concentrated management attention on the continuous improvement of their business processes is the fact that both sectors are high-volume, rapid-moving and low-margin businesses. In that environment a penny or even a fraction of a penny saved without sacrificing quality can make millions. Equally such businesses just could not survive for very long if they ignored the levels of waste (cost of quality) that were found and ignored in most other industries. M & S and Sainsbury did not need the Japanese or the quality gurus to concentrate their minds on that aspect of internal quality. Both these companies have now reached the level of sophistication that they know almost the next day which of their hundreds of outlets have too few or too many cans of baked beans or specific size panties on their shelves. Knowledge is one thing, but action, communication and empowerment to act by individual managers is an essential part of their successful cultures.

The continual search for improvement in every aspect of their operations to 'gain an edge' has led the best retailers to invest heavily in automation, in training and in extending their sphere of influence far beyond the borders of their own operations. They also invest heavily in competitive evaluation and research on an international scale. Many of them now operate as international giants.

Retailers were among the first to move from relatively sophisticated mechanical and electrical processes to harness the power of computers. The author well remembers, as long ago as the late fifties, that the so-called 'management science applications' were dominated by the questing needs of the retail and distribution industries. The average shopper has little comprehension of the technical sophistication and deep knowledge of their own behaviour that lie behind bar codes and the 'point of sale' devices that they witness in action at every checkout. Incidentally, the very fact that the equipment is called 'point of sale' indicates the level of customer focus in retailing; in other industries they might have been seen as accounting or inventory control devices. There can be little argument that the retail sector uses the power of computer technology in both managing day-to-day operations, and as aids to long-term decision-making, to a far greater extent than almost any other industry.

The management and development of people and their potential is a more mixed picture, even in the best of the retailers. The relatively high investment in education and training has already been noted. In truth this is almost wholly dedicated to managers, potential managers and other permanent staff. But they represent only a proportion of the people involved. Like the hotel and catering sector, retailing employs a very high proportion of people classified as temporary. This results from another characteristic of the industry known as 'seasonality'. For a large number of retailers seasonality exists on two planes: the obvious Christmas peaks and the weekly buying pattern of shoppers.

Seasonality causes a variety of problems for management, not least of which is the employment of people. Each location will employ a nucleus of permanent staff. The annual and weekly peaks of trade are bridged by temporary staff; on key days they may outnumber the permanent staff. This creates a difficult dilemma for management who are attempting to meet the needs of customers. On the one day that the customer deals with the business, the primary contact may not be sufficiently trained and therefore will not delight them. Their business depends on continually delighting the customer but can they really afford to train all their temporary staff adequately? Disney would argue that if they really intend to delight every customer it would be suicide not to train every individual in the organisation, permanent and temporary. There are no easy answers when the temptation to compromise on quality rears its head. However, the leading retailers have two advantages: people want to work for them and they have clearly defined the requirements of each process. Both go to the root of people motivation and a performing workforce.

Quality concepts must be rooted in the organisation. But to achieve quality continuously in the eyes of the customer that is not enough. Every organisation is impacted by external factors such as the quality of their suppliers. The leading retailers have demonstrated this simple truth from the beginning. Figure 8 illustrates a simplified diagram of the retail chain. The reality is much more complex. The organisation itself will be represented by perhaps several hundred of 'our own houses'. Each will be supplied by a large number of primary suppliers who are separate companies with their own problems and cultures. The vast number of individual products have to be distributed from the suppliers to a multitude of locations – all at exactly the time and in the quantity required and also to the quality required.

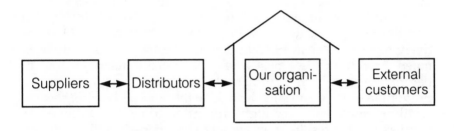

Figure 8. The retail distribution chain

The major retailers have devoted a substantial proportion of their management resource to ensuring that this chain operates effectively to satisfy the final external customer. Some own and control their distributors but most combine an element of their own distribution with outside distribution companies. They actively involve themselves, some say interfere, in the management of their distributors and suppliers. This of course is an exercise of their buying power and many commentators have criticised the way they use such power. Some retailers certainly have caused havoc in this arena but usually to their own long-term disadvantage. The best have usually built long-term 'associations' with their distributors and suppliers in which all work as part of a team to the advantage of both. Marks and Spencer are a leading example of this approach and their relationships and achievements with suppliers have been well documented. It can be said that in yet another area of industrial and commercial success the retail industry has shown the way.

Distribution is the 'Cinderella' industry in the eyes of the general public. Even this chapter has used the term as an appendage to the retail sector. When described as the haulage or transportation industry it gains some credence in its own right, but even then its image is centred around a false idea of trucks and drivers. Few realise that it uses some of the most sophisticated computer techniques available and employs a high proportion of the very best managers. Distribution is the logistical heart of every economically successful nation. The major problem facing Eastern Europe and the states of the former Soviet Union is the failure of their distribution network.

The importance of logistics or distribution has been consistently ignored throughout history. Military history concentrates on the instant decisions of battlefield commanders. General Patton is extolled as one of the great battlefield commanders and motivators of combat troops, yet probably his greatest military achievement, unsurpassed at the time, was the logistical repositioning, within twenty-four hours, of a whole army corps at the Battle of the Bulge. The highly professional Wehrmacht which had swept through Europe was finally defeated by logistics. Its magnificently-led Panzer divisions stood impotent at the gates of Moscow, foiled not by snow but because its supply of fuel and ammunition was largely based on horse-drawn transport. In the vital days it could not move fast enough to beat the weather and exploit its strategic advantage.

The art of war is to position the right number of troops and weapons at the right place at the right time. Only then does motivation and the skill of individual soldiers count. The quality of tanks, artillery and all the sophisticated weaponry of modern warfare count for little if there is no fuel to drive them or ammunition to fire.

You can measure the efficiency of a modern army by its logistical strength or more prosaically by *trucks*. The same is true of industry. The effectiveness of the retailing sector and most other human endeavours in the modern state ultimately depends on the efficient use of trucks. Some of the characteristics of the transportation industry will be examined in Chapter 11.

The reader may consider that this chapter has viewed the retail and distribution industry with rose-tinted spectacles. There is some truth in this, but the balance between service and manufacturing had to be redressed. At its very best this market sector is a lesson to all, way ahead of usual practice. It can also be the worst, by any comparative standard. Even the best, faced with the problems of growth, need to use the concepts of TQM to maintain their competitive advantage and ensure that their culture lives on with new employees. The author, as a consultant in these concepts, will listen very carefully to the market leaders, but is tempted to wring the necks of many others in the retail and distribution industry.

10. LOCAL AUTHORITIES

'Government, even in its best state, is but a necessary evil; in its worst state, an intolerable one.' *Thomas Paine, 1776*

'I thought the best to do was to settle up those little local difficulties.' *Harold Macmillan, 1958*

Local government and in particular urban authorities are in difficulty throughout the Western world. Whatever the power or decisions of central government, the local authorities have the direct contact with the people being governed. The reactions of the people are most evident where it actually happens – in the local community. In an age of division, turmoil and change the local community is not a comfortable place to exercise responsibility and authority.

The evidence of the breakdown of local authority is clear to see. Major cities such as New York and Liverpool are, in commercial terms, bankrupt. Our television screens are regularly dominated by scenes of burning streets with looting and rampaging rioters from as far apart as Los Angeles and Bristol. Large areas of cities around the world have become virtual no-go areas for law-abiding citizens. Muggers, rapists and murderers stalk the streets or lie in wait in parks and gardens. Drugs and deprivation are commonplace and seem almost ignored. The apparent collapse of law and order or the ability to exercise authority are not confined to major conurbations. The truckers and farmers of France, the neo-fascists of Germany and the mafiosa of southern Italy demonstrate that the malaise is present whatever the size of the community. It is just more concentrated in the big cities.

Local authorities are caught on the horns of a dilemma. As the cost of maintaining the fabric and services of towns and cities inexorably rises they demand higher local taxes or rates from the inhabitants and increasing support from central government. Unfortunately, those most capable of paying increasing taxes are fleeing the urban areas to chase a better way of life. At the same time in some cities the electoral majorities are almost exempt from taxes and elect representatives to spend more on alleviating their problems. The wicked spiral of profligate spending continues, in many cases exacerbated by militant idealogues. Margaret Thatcher's ill-fated poll tax was intended to bring responsibility back to the local scene in the UK by insisting that everyone made some contribution towards local expenditure. Governments faced with growing budget deficits have reduced their contributions wherever possible. As a result local authorities are in constant conflict with central government and large sectors of their own communities.

Within the town halls elected representatives are divided from their officials, staff and associated authorities such as the police. Along with the growing loss of public esteem the morale of public employees is falling and their union representatives, often politically motivated, seem powerless. Of course there are exceptions and many local authorities are models of good management. It should also be said that thousands of elected representatives really care about their local communities and make major contributions to local life. All in all local government does not provide the most propitious environment for the introduction of TQM and the pursuit of continuous improvement. However, the *need* is painfully obvious.

In the bleak environment described, local government representatives and officials are too often so busy fighting fires that they have no time to reflect on issues like management style and future visions. This situation is also not uncommon in industry and commerce. Generally it is the successful organisations that are not satisfied with the status quo and have the time and confidence to strive to be even better. Some organisations have turned to quality only when they stared disaster in the face. The Xerox Corporation is a prime example of a company lulled by long unrivalled success into a false sense of security; then suddenly almost overwhelmed by fierce competition from Japanese copier companies, they woke up – just in time. They rose like a phoenix from the ashes with a total dedication to quality. Local authorities have no reason to be satisfied with the status quo but there is also no reason why quality improvement cannot help a community organisation, just as it has for many business organisations.

In truth many local authorities have started down the long road to excellence. Despite the dismal picture painted above UK local authorities are well ahead in world terms in applying quality standards such as BS 5750 (ISO 9000). Several authorities in both the UK and the USA have established major quality initiatives in partnership with their private sector neighbours. This has enabled them to share expertise and foster a new era of collaboration between the public and private sector. In practice this has led to a working collaboration to establish a clean environment and encouraged the whole community to take quality of life seriously, most usually through addressing the 'green issues'. Interestingly, it has also made political sense for the representatives.

Local government, by its very nature, does have one advantage that is relevant to the implementation of TQM – namely, that it is localised. This is a similar inherent advantage that the smaller company has over its big brother. They both have shorter and more meaningful lines of communication, an environment more suited to developing a common shared culture and above all the organisation is closer to the customer. Though local government employees share many attitudes with those in central government they can have little doubt that their real customer is the local community. Local bureaucrats can sometimes convey the impression that local citizens are barely tolerated, but the fact is that the local electorate is too close to wholly ignore.

Closeness to customer or community is a key issue. In that light it is interesting to observe that of those local authorities in England that are investing in quality initiatives a substantial proportion are controlled by the Liberal Party. The reason is perhaps the organisational nature of the Liberals rather than deep-rooted philosophy. The membership of the Liberal Party is organised through loosely linked local associations rather than through a cohesive national organisation. With limited power in Westminster, they have sought to grow their influence through 'community politics'. With some notable exceptions they have been relatively successful.

These political patterns are all relatively recent. Before the nineteen sixties the Conservative Party implicitly took a similar approach to local government. Outside the big cities a large proportion of local authorities in England were governed by Ratepayers' and Residents' Associations which were in all but name largely Conservative. Nevertheless, they felt independent and were locally orientated. The post-war strength of the Labour Party led to a climate of centralism and the increasing involvement of central government in local affairs. Local Labour-controlled authorities became almost an extension of their Party in Westminster. The Conservatives sought to combat this growing 'politicisation' of local government by their own political centralisation. Following the poll tax debacle and the new climate of decentralisation there are growing signs that Conservative local authorities are seeking much more local independence.

From the quality standpoint in service to the community there is a real need to devolve power locally – to bring decisions closer to the customer and encourage a greater involvement from members of the community. However, that is not just an issue of party political organisation. Most of the changes noted earlier in the chapter on Central Government are required in the local arena. The local community also needs *less government*. TQM could be a powerful change agent to bring about this evolution.

11. MOVING PEOPLE AND GOODS

'Fly away Peter, fly away Paul
Come back Peter, come back Paul.'
Anonymous plea to the airline industry.

'It was the wrong kind of snow.' *British Rail spokesman.*

'We regret to announce.' *All transportation training manuals – Lesson One.*

Moving people and goods is the mission of the transportation industry. Both can and are being moved continuously by road, rail, air and water. Individual organisations within the industry usually are differentiated by the methods they use to transport people and goods – airlines, shipping companies, railways or railroads and truck or bus companies. Most companies in the industry move both people and goods but there is a strong differentiation, in the eyes of the public, between those who predominantly move one or the other.

Public protest and scorn is most often directed at those companies that predominantly move people. The obvious reason for that focus is that the public are the people being moved. Parcels and crates are not usually vocal and if they occasionally seem to be then they are a security risk. But that is not the only reason for this concern. There is evidence that there is a substantial difference in performance between the two types of carrier, which is not to the advantage of the people movers. The difference stems from the strength of focus on the real nature of their businesses and on the extent that they understand their customers.

It is interesting to compare how both types of carrier promote their services to their prospective customers. Compare the advertising of airlines with that of the international couriers such as Federal Express or DHL. The difference in approach seems to be similar whether on television, hoardings or in magazines.

Delta was highlighted earlier in this book but most airline advertising is similar in concept. They expect the public to be tempted (as they themselves appear to be) by the so-called 'romance of flying' – a perception of the customer which is well out of date. There are three commonly repeated elements in nearly all of these advertisements. First the beautifully liveried plane resplendent in azure blue skies with the slightest hint of cotton wool puffs of white cloud. This is usually supported by an interior with a smartly dressed and groomed air stewardess delicately serving a 'gourmet' meal, apparently with all the time in the world. There is a choice for the third element, probably depending on preponderance of routes of the particular airline. The choice is between a backdrop of an exotic destination or a close-up of their new specially designed seat. Very little of this is really related to the normal traveller's perception of air travel or really differentiates the carrier.

A brief analysis of these elements of airline advertising will demonstrate how far removed these images are from reality and the real desires of travellers. Increasingly the only differentiation in the airplane is the livery; a Boeing 747 is a Boeing 747, however it is painted. This applies equally to the interiors and the seats. With the possible exception of first class, most travellers' experience of 'gourmet' food service is harassed stewards attempting to serve several hundred trays of processed food in limited time and space. As for exotic destinations, or any destinations for that matter, they are rarely chosen on the basis of which airline flies there – at most that would be the traveller's second question.

Perhaps the most extreme of all the fantasy promotions was that used for some time on television by Air Canada. It showed an airliner standing on the runway at its destination with muffled sounds of laughter and music coming from the open doors with not a passenger in sight. The message was 'Nobody wants to leave an Air Canada flight'. Amusing, but it is difficult to imagine anything further from the desires of prospective passengers.

Most airlines are making promises that have little meaning, probably because they dare not make the promises the traveller would really appreciate.

The more prosaic international couriers that move only goods use their advertisements to make promises which in the main they do keep. As it happens, they are almost the same promises that the traveller would like from the airlines. They are not tempted by romance, so they concentrate their advertising and, more important, the operation of their business on what the customer really wants. They know that the customer (and even less so the parcel) is not really interested in the type of plane, or what's for lunch. Their promotion concentrates on delivering the goods with absolute certainty on time, to the right address and in perfect condition. They also ensure that the journey is easy to book, that all the paperwork is correct and easy to understand, that the parcel is picked up and delivered with little or no hassle to the sender and the receiver, and that they will compensate the customer if they fail to keep those promises.

As a frequent traveller, the author knows of two airlines that come close to the standards of the couriers. These are Virgin Atlantic and Emirates and he has been told by others of two far eastern airlines which meet similar standards. Business and first-class travellers on these airlines are picked up from their homes by chauffeured limousines and similarly transported to their final destination from the arrival airport. Booking and check-in are fast and convenient with the number of handling staff commensurate with the number of travellers. The cabin staff are well trained and groomed. All manner of extra little services are provided on board, some admittedly gimmicks, but all show imagination and real thought about the traveller. The author has never known any of these flights to leave or arrive late for other than extreme weather conditions. Though their economy-class flights do not include this level of service they are superior to those of most other airlines. They are both customer-focused airlines.

Apart from service there is one other similarity between these airlines and the leading international couriers. All have implemented and are maintaining major quality initiatives to ensure that they retain their competitive edge. It is notable that they also seem to be able to negotiate better service from the airport authorities.

In recent years a large number of airlines have turned to quality to improve their service and to attempt to differentiate themselves from the competition. Unfortunately, most of them are amongst the companies that have experienced the disappointments noted in Chapter 5. They have either not maintained the impetus or settled for the customer care 'quick fix' route. Two notable exceptions which have maintained TQM initiatives throughout their operations are KLM and SAS. The latter company attributes the dramatic turnround in its fortunes to their dedication to their quality effort.

The dramatic growth of road and air travel had a calamitous impact on rail travel. For many years the railways have languished in the doldrums. Throughout the world few were able to remain profitable within the private sector. Most are either nationalised or receiving massive government subsidies. The 'romance of steam' is gone for ever but there are strong signs of a resurgence for the transport of both people and goods by rail. Two-hundred-mile-an-hour TGV's and Golden Bullets hurtle across France and Japan. Britain has more express trains travelling at well over one hundred miles an hour than any other country in the world. The British government has also announced plans to privatise elements of its rail network and services. As the road networks around conurbations steadily become giant parking lots the railways may have a golden future. A pity that the advice of the great engineer Brunel last century to standardise on the broad gauge was not followed: it is easier to widen motorways than railways.

Quality of service will be the main driver if rail travel is to compete aggressively with air and road travel. But the railways face a lot of problems. Firstly, there are three distinct markets attempting to share many of the same facilities: fast inter-city networks, slow continually stopping commuter and rival networks and substantial movements of goods varying from containerised components to the bulk carriage of anything from oil to grain. Each has to be handled in a different way though often using the same tracks, signalling equipment and stations. This all requires massive investment in modernisation to meet new requirements and to repair the years of neglect of rolling stock and facilities. In densely populated Europe and Japan fast inter-city networks are profitable and provide real competition. Conversely, commuter networks require large numbers of expensive rolling stock and staff for two bursts of ninety minutes at each end of the day and for weekdays only. It is competitively impossible, as things stand at the moment, to charge an economic fare for commuter networks, which are therefore heavily subsidised in most countries. Nevertheless great strides are being made to solve these problems.

Conrail, headquartered in Philadelphia, USA, has used a total quality drive throughout its operations to transform a quasi-nationalised debt-laden railroad into a highly profitable and efficient private company. Perhaps that is due to Pennsylvania's historical love of railroads.

Mention was made previously of the UK government's introduction of a Citizens' Charter for varying sections of the public sector. As part of that process British Rail published a Passengers' Charter with a subtitle of 'Raising The Standard' in early 1992. The Charter is a statement of their commitment to provide a high-quality service for their passengers. It spells out a number of objectives including the standards they are determined to achieve, keeping the public informed of their progress against the standards, linking the prices of season tickets to performance on individual routes and providing details of the compensation they will make to passengers if they fail to meet the standards. According to the Charter they want to give their passengers:

- A safe, punctual and reliable train service.
- Clean stations and clean trains.
- Friendly and efficient service.
- Clear and up-to-date information.
- A fair and satisfactory response if things go wrong.

They state that the Charter is only a beginning. They aim to improve standards over time, and to develop and improve their services in a way that will clearly show their intent to care for their passengers. The full Charter defines the standards of service for everything from buying tickets to train punctuality. Each Region of the whole rail network for the UK has also published its own subdivision of the Charter as it applies to their services. It's a magnificent start but they are going to need an organisation-wide TQM process to achieve their objectives.

All forms of transportation require substantial facilities and supporting services, often supplied by another company or owned by the public sector. Planes require airports and traffic control networks. Trains need track, signalling networks, stations and a host of other facilities. Trucks and cars require roads, traffic signals, parking space and clear signs. Ships require docks, a variety of loading and unloading equipment and their own signalling systems such as lighthouses and radar stations. Most of these services also require coordination between rival carriers and other modes of transport to ensure connections. Most major journeys involve two or three modes of travel and the use of different companies within any one mode. Again, a large proportion of journeys involves a host of other services such as catering, communications, travel agents and car rental which are not immediately thought of as part of the transportation industry.

The myriad of related services is the Achilles' heel of the transportation industry. Most airlines have safe planes and competent pilots and passengers readily accept that fact. The public generally feels secure about rail travel but it is not so certain about sea travel; recent ferry disasters may account for some uneasiness but in general it is the turbulent uncontrolled nature of the sea itself that creates anxiety. For similar reasons there are anxieties about road travel caused by the state of the carriageway and the proximity to other 'amateur' drivers. However, passengers are usually satisfied by the prime service of the carrier. The vast majority of complaints from travellers emanate from the other services not always under the control of the prime carrier.

Many prime carriers do work on improving the quality of their own service and to some extent the quality provided by immediate suppliers such as caterers. However, they all too often shrug their shoulders about the standard of service provided by others in the journey network. Yet the passenger will reflect on the quality of the whole journey and the surrounding environment. The passenger who has waited a long time for a piece of luggage which eventually arrives damaged will not think kindly of the airline which transported him, but at many airports the airline has no control over baggage handling. This is an important quality dimension which should concern all movers of people and goods.

In the retail and distribution industries we have seen that the market leaders take a great deal of trouble ensuring that every element of the total service to their customers is considered. They work closely with all their suppliers and connecting services. This even extends into the public sector. The owners of supermarkets will not only negotiate for planning permission with the local authorities but persuade the authorities to rebuild the local road network servicing their site. The transportation industry has to have the same attitude. That is what the word 'Total' means in both TQM and TCI.

12. NATIONAL HEALTH SERVICE

'The National Health Service is the jewel in the crown...' *Election debate, 1992.*

'My job is not to find out what the patient wants, but to tell him what he needs.' *Anonymous hospital consultant.*

Until recently the two largest employers in the world were the Red Army of the Soviet Union and the National Health Service (NHS) of the UK. Now the NHS would appear to have that doubtful privilege to itself. However, that is not quite so dramatic in comparison to other countries as it might appear. In all the developed countries healthcare is now the biggest single industry. The difference is that in Britain the vast majority of that industry is still in the public sector, though it is worth noting that private healthcare is growing and, in some sectors of the NHS, becoming a strong competitor.

The NHS is a vast and complex organisation involving all the acute and other services of hospitals, general practitioners, dentists and a large array of community healthcare services. Though opticians and retail pharmacists are in the private sector a substantial proportion of their income is funded through the NHS. The NHS itself is funded in the main from general taxation but increasingly patients are having to contribute to the cost of drugs, glasses and dental care unless they can show need.

Funding healthcare and providing an improved standard of patient service is a major political issue in Britain and indeed in most countries. The combination of an ageing population, the escalating costs of drugs and the advances in medical technology has put an almost intolerable strain on the national budget. At the end of the seventies the NHS was at crisis point and the concept of universal healthcare as a basic right to all citizens was in doubt.

Despite the continuing political furore the NHS *has* demonstrably improved its service to the community over the last decade and shows signs that it will continue to improve. In the context of the previous history of the NHS and in the midst of a major economic recession it is an amazing achievement that a government can have the confidence to remain committed to the principle of providing a comprehensive national health service *free* to *all* of its people at the moment of need. Some still dismiss this as political rhetoric but it is fundamentally true and could be matched by few other nations. Many UK citizens only become aware of their advantages when they face a medical emergency in another country. The British have much to be proud of in the NHS and its gigantic army of caring employees.

The change in the NHS has not come easily and it is not yet completed. Under the umbrella of the 'NHS Reforms', driven by a strong and committed government, the NHS is undergoing a revolution. Change does not come easily to a massive bureaucratic organisation with entrenched professional and labour union fortresses. Each can summon up enough emotion to believe sincerely that it is defending a great institution and the rights of patients when in reality they are resisting change from outdated traditional practices or battling to maintain their own power base. In short, the last decade has been a period of upheaval, change and conflict within the NHS and in the political life of the nation.

The UK government initiated the revolution in the NHS when it commissioned a series of studies into the future of the NHS in all its aspects. In 1983 the most influential study, the NHS Management Inquiry, known as the Griffiths Report after its Chairman, Sir Roy Griffiths, was published. This was followed by a number of other reports, including 'Working for Patients' in 1989, which have formed the basis for the reforms and incidentally highlighted the importance of quality assurance and total quality management. The importance of quality was also reinforced by the World Health Organisation's 'Targets for Health for All' published in 1985. The NHS also has its own 'Citizens' Charter' spelling out what patients should expect.

There are three basic elements to the reform of the NHS. The most fundamental is the split between purchasers and providers, creating an *internal* market for healthcare. District health authorities, which used to manage the hospitals, are now budgeted as purchasers. Their task is to evaluate the health needs of their communities and then to purchase healthcare to meet those needs, not necessarily from the hospitals in their area or those they previously managed. Hospitals are the providers but will only be guaranteed funds to the limit of the contracts they can win from the purchasers. In other words, the money goes with the patient. However, money is not the only arbiter. The contracts from the purchasers must also define the quality standards they expect from the provider.

The other two basic elements are related to the first. A further devolution of funding for the NHS, bringing it nearer to the patient and creating more internal market choice, is provided by allowing, indeed encouraging, general practitioners to manage their own budgets and becoming to a large extent purchasers. This reform met with strong resistance from the doctor's union (the British Medical Association) but since the 1992 general election it seems to be finding favour with an increasing number of general practitioners. The other reform encouraged hospitals and community services to become self-governing trusts. The latter proved the most controversial of all the reforms, bringing a storm of political protest and accusing the government of privatising the NHS through the back door. It is difficult to see how this move could be interpreted as returning hospitals to the private sector when the funding and contracts of service are determined by the Department of Health through the district health authorities and general practitioners.

All this turmoil has put a considerable strain on the management of the NHS and has exacerbated internal strife between the administrators and the medical staff. In fact, it has involved the NHS in a complete change in the culture of the organisation and its managerial approach. As a result TQM is coming to the fore in many hospitals, health authorities and community service units. The new emphasis on quality of care and service with a developing orientation around the patient is allied to the power of TQM as a change agent.

The task of managing a hospital today has become exceedingly complex. On a daily basis administrators are charged with making critical decisions in areas involving financial resources, shortages of technical and clinical personnel, admissions, waiting lists, computers and other highly technical equipment, standards of care, security and clinical issues – not to mention the problems of litigation. There are undoubtedly some very good NHS managers, but the majority have had no experience of the commercial realities of contracts. They are under immense pressures of both knowledge and time. A historical underinvestment in management training and the traditional mistrust between clinicians and administrators are part of the problem.

TQM can be seen as a mixed blessing in the midst of a host of other changes and surrounded by problems. As an old adage goes: 'It is difficult to concentrate on draining the swamp when you are up to your neck in alligators.' John Morgan, Director of Quality Assurance at the Department of Social Policy, University of Birmingham, states that NHS employees view TQM with a great amount of cynicism. 'Where is the time to identify corporate aims and values, train and equip all levels of staff, and assess and respond to users' needs? Why should money desperately needed for running hospitals and purchasing equipment go to another management fad?' But not all NHS managers view TQM in this way. As David O'Neill, General Manager of the Trafford Health Authority, states: 'Total quality is not a separate thing that sits in a room elsewhere. It is interwoven with all the other issues that are being dealt with.'

Cynicism about the NHS has always been concerned about quality; they are by no stretch of the imagination 'Johnny-come-late-ly's' to the subject. Clinical and nursing standards are constantly reviewed, developed and audited. Indeed, to some extent this has created a resistance to the implementation of 'outside industry' concepts such as TQM on the basis of both 'but we are different' and the feeling that they already have quality. Three main confusions appear to inhibit full comprehension of the role of TQM in healthcare. They can be summarised as:

- To improve quality we need more money; there isn't any more money; or, alternatively, the government must give us more money.
- Its relevance to both administration and to clinical practice (a long divide in the NHS).
- The difference between outcome quality and process quality. This was illustrated in Chapter 6.

The Healthcare Quality Model (Figure 9) attempts in diagrammatic form to tackle the last two confusions but does little to help in the first case.

The money argument has to some extent been solved. The Government did provide several million pounds to fund a series of TQM and other quality initiatives to evaluate their effectiveness in assisting the reforms. An evaluation study has also been funded to report on all these projects for the benefit of the whole service. TQM is alive and kicking in many areas of the NHS.

An American healthcare consultant now working in Britain, Nancy Dixon, commenting on the general state of quality in the NHS, has said; 'There is a general and correct feeling that doctors and nurses give their best and do an excellent job, but that they have little or no say in the financial management and expenditure of the budget. This contributes to making it difficult to implement formal systems to monitor quality in an environment unused to quality systems. In the US, where healthcare operates on a commercial basis, hospitals are required by law to have a quality programme. Recent NHS reforms require medical audit and encourage quality initiatives but, as yet, there is no formal requirement for a quality programme.' This is a fair assessment though one might comment that the

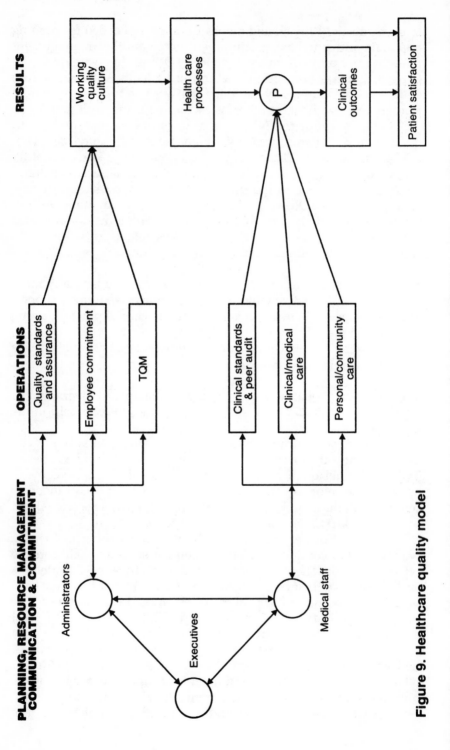

Figure 9. Healthcare quality model

majority of quality systems in American hospitals fall far short of TQM as described in this book.

However, some British hospitals have become quite sophisticated in their use of TQM techniques. The St Helier Hospital in the Merton and Sutton District, a southern suburb of London, is a case in point. Figures 10 to 13 illustrate their use of analysis diagrams and demonstrate their concentration on processes. They also show the practical use of the forms described in Chapter 3. Figure 10 illustrates the activities and requirements involved in scheduling an operating theatre. The following figures trace the process flow through a number of subprocesses of the overall process of admitting a patient. We shall see more of the work at St Helier's Hospital later in this book.

The NHS is embracing quality and there is substantial evidence that more and more authorities and hospitals will turn to TQM over the coming years. Quality management consultants are swarming all over the NHS and individual quality seminars for the service are packed. Many of those consultants will be disappointed because they do not properly understand the nature of the animal. The NHS can be likened to a great big club; they gather together and 'gossip' or, perhaps more fairly, share experiences. They are likely to find their own answers and develop their own variants of TQM and TCI which could surprise other industries. There are many highly intelligent, enquiring and caring people in the National Health Service.

We end this chapter with an American example. A healthcare leader in the USA in both performance and commitment to quality, the Baptist Memorial Hospital of Memphis, Tennessee, used the following statistics to demonstrate the importance of zero defects:

What does 99.9 per cent quality mean? In the USA it would mean:

- One hour of unsafe drinking water per day

- 500 incorrect surgical operations performed each week

- Two unsafe landings at O'Hare Airport, Chicago, each day

- 19,000 newborn babies dropped at birth by doctors each year

- 16,000 lost pieces of mail each hour

- 22,000 cheques deducted from the wrong account each hour

- 22,000 incorrect prescriptions each year

- Your heart fails to beat 32,000 times each year

A powerful argument to convince people to take quality seriously!

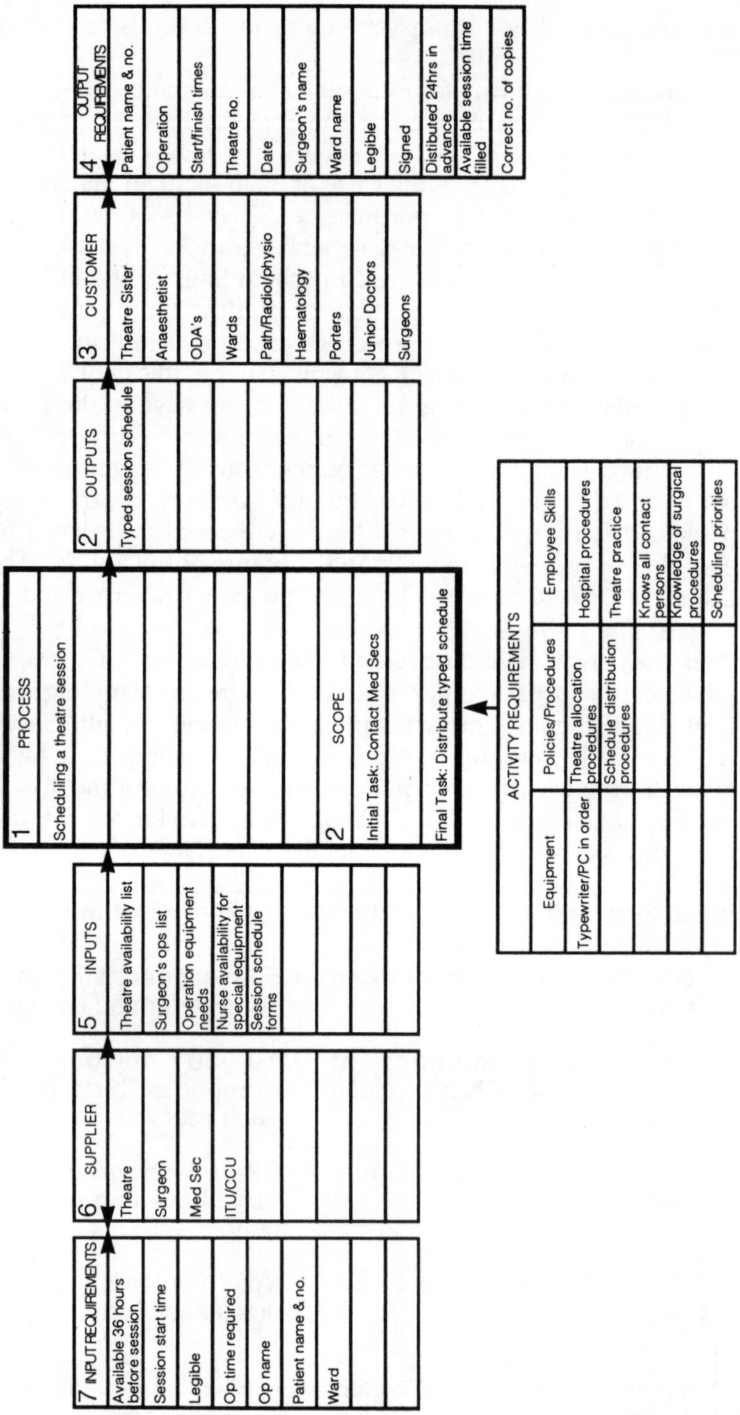

Figure 10.
Acute Services Unit —
activity analysis diagram

Figure 11. Process flow analysis

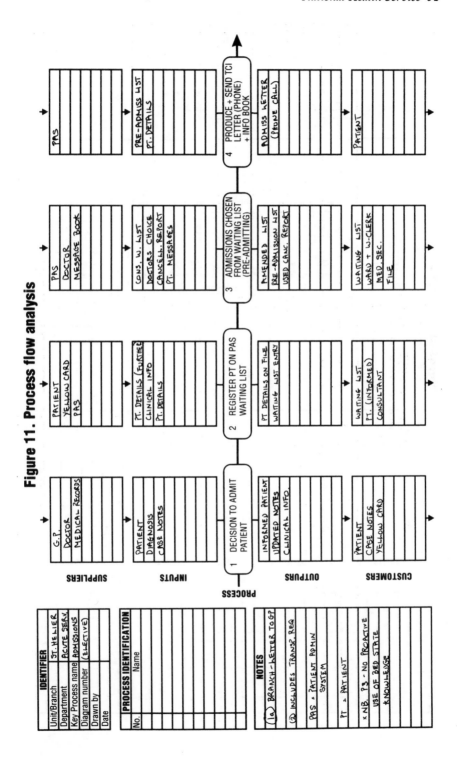

Figure 12. Process flow analysis

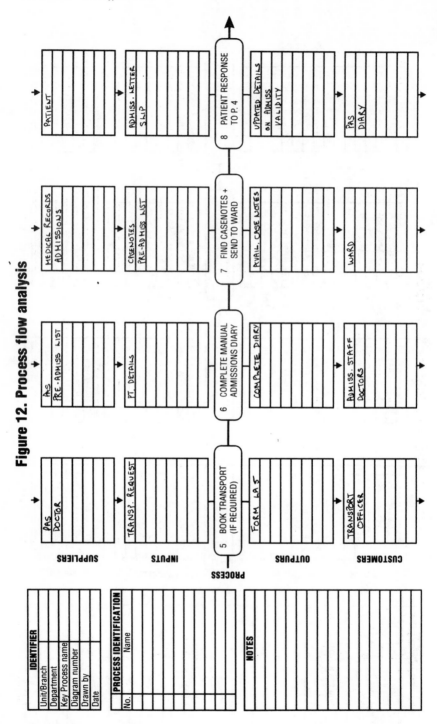

Figure 13. Process flow analysis

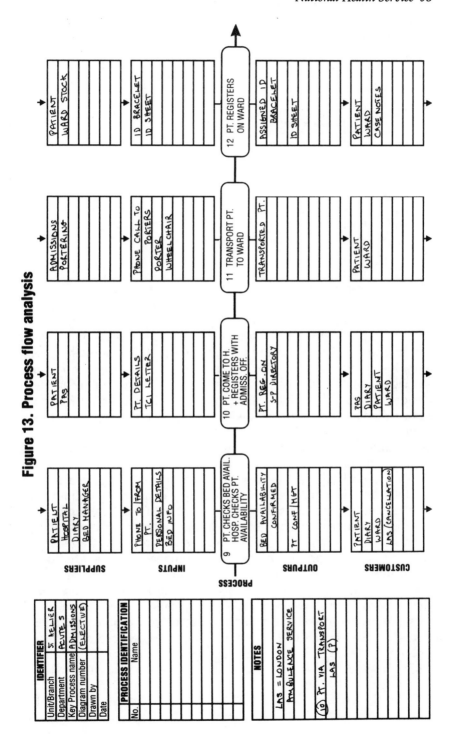

13. CONSULTANTS

'We will measure our contribution more by the quality of service rendered than by whether we make a good living out of it.'
Arthur E Andersen, founder of the firm in 1913.

The word consultant covers a multitude of specialist advisers and some would say sins. Many specialists revel in the term consultant. Others look on the term with some disdain and would rather be known as professionals. To some extent there is a division between those who merely advise and those who actually do something as a service for their clients. But this is a tenuous division, for many management consultants do implement their advice or recommendations, and the highest accolade in the British medical profession is to be called a consultant. Yet lawyers, architects, surveyors and academics would hate to be considered mere consultants. However, in this chapter the word consultant will be used generically to cover all these practitioners and professionals.

The second half of the twentieth century has become a testing time for the consultancy professions. As the demand for and reliance on their services has grown familiarity has bred if not contempt then at least questioning. The general public, usually in the shape of clients, has begun to question the level of service they are receiving from consultants, and even their basic competence. When buildings fall down, convicted people are later found to be innocent, house purchasers are 'gazumped' or cheated, auditors do not notice that the pension funds have been stolen and people die because of a silly mistake by a surgeon there is bound to be concern. The resulting decline in deference to the professional has been dramatic. Their opinions or advice, once almost sacrosanct, are no longer automatically accepted. The educated layman is ever more ready to challenge his professional adviser.

With this change in attitude has come the rise of litigation, which threatens the very existence of many professional organisations. A high proportion of professionals operate under partnership law, which does not limit liability; so all their personal wealth is at risk. It started in the litigious nation USA but is now rapidly growing in Europe. Complaints once blocked or held in check by the monopolistic practices of professional associations such as the Law Society and the British Medical Association are fought out in the law courts. When lawyers begin to sue lawyers there has been a radical change in the professional climate. When a major accounting firm can be sued for more than three million dollars there is fear in the air. The cost of indemnity assurance against these risks is soaring and some professional groups such as architects are spending up to a quarter of their fees to provide some protection.

This whole situation has led to two discernible reactions, one external and the other internal to the professions. The external reaction is a growing demand for a reform of the professions, backed by legislation if necessary. Internally, an increasing number of partnerships and organisations are turning to quality assurance and even TQM, both as a form of saviour and to help them enter the new competitive world.

Professional bodies were formed ostensibly for the protection of the public but in many cases they developed into closed shops for the protection of professional privilege. Originally long and expensive training was the entry requirement to ensure the best possible service to the client or patient and to enhance the standing of the particular specialism. This was usually followed by a number of years of apprenticeship or 'articles' at a minimal level of remuneration. The traditional reason for this indenture was to inculcate professional ethics and skills into the budding consultant but in reality it provided cheap labour for the professional partnership. Naturally, those who have attained the peak through the 'school of hard knocks' were not going to allow others to dilute their pre-eminence or find an easier way to the top. The professional bodies became established monopolies of closed-shop middle-class unions and they were joined by quasi-professional bodies to protect less august sectors of professionalism such as insurance brokers and estate agents.

As might be expected, they became hidebound traditionalists wary of competition or criticism. An interesting example of these attitudes, directly relating to quality, comes from The Law Society. Pressed to encourage law firms to seek BS 5750 registration by some advanced members, The Law Society published a quality briefing that stated: 'Too many firms fall below the standard required for BS 5750 as to practice management care. Promotion of BS 5750 might raise public expectation unrealistically.' Unfortunately for The Law

Society and other professional bodies, public expectation is all too realistic; they want reform.

Margaret Thatcher was a radical Prime Minister. Once she had successfully curbed the power of the workers' trade unions she turned her attention to the middle-class trade or professional unions. She found the professionals a much tougher proposition. They used every 'trick of the trade' to resist the attack on their monopolistic practices and to break down the rigid demarcation lines. A legal profession divided between barristers and solicitors; a medical profession divided between surgeons, general practitioners and nurses. This was 'class warfare' and Mrs Thatcher was seen to be turning against her own supporters: her own class. The professional bodies were able to mobilise support amongst their own members in Parliament. As a result each proposed reform was stifled at birth or had most of the teeth drawn before it reached the Statute Book. But the pressures for reform and the strong wind of competition may prove too strong to resist for ever.

The successful pressures for reform may come in the shape of a Trojan Horse, from within. Intelligent and far-seeing partners and managers can see the way the wind is blowing. They want to succeed in an increasingly competitive world and they recognise that the most likely key to success will be provided by continuously improving the quality of their services to their clients. They also recognise that the perceptions of their clients and patients have changed and if they are to meet the rising expectations of clients they must eliminate the traditional restrictions and tear down the fortress walls of demarcation. Many have already turned to TQM and this trend looks likely to accelerate.

A quality pioneer in the legal profession is the Manchester-based international firm of solicitors Parmone March Pearson (PMP). In 1991 PMP became the first legal firm to be awarded BS 5750 certification and it is deeply committed to TQM. The systems it has implemented aim to ensure that the supporting office systems, incorporating all aspects of the firm's practice, produce an efficient and quality-conscious working environment. The certification does not guarantee the quality of legal advice, but it assures clients that they will receive a quality service.

PMP Partner Andrew Gordon Simpkin, writing about their progress, said that what was surprising was that 'nine-tenths of the good practices in each of the departments are the same, regardless of the type of work. Good practices apply to any job, whether in commercial or private practice.' The company now leads the profession in providing a service to a recognised and assessed quality level, in addition to The Law Society's code of practice, proving that the principles of service quality can apply to lawyers.

PMP provide a powerful lesson to commerce and industry as well as all consultants. Many commercial organisations have difficulty in involving the specialists or knowledge workers into their overall TQM processes. Specialists such as lawyers, actuaries, doctors, research and development scientists and many others see themselves as creative individuals and therefore outside the process of general improvement. Those with that attitude all too often cannot accept that these concepts apply to them. Management consultancies face a similar syndrome in the sense that the individual consultants, spending a lot of time away dispensing advice to executives and others, return to their own organisation and have a tendency to see themselves or subconsciously act as prima donnas. When a substantial and successful firm of lawyers can so wholeheartedly embrace the concepts of quality and TQM it provides a shining example for all specialists and consultants.

A world-class quality organisation committed to the concepts discussed in this book are Arthur Andersen, the international accounting firm. That is perhaps not surprising in view of the quotation from their founder which heads this chapter. But very few organisations successfully maintain the ethos of their founder (this is even true of churches) over some nine decades. The author believes that a key element of continued success in their field is to be found in the importance they place on the 'values' of the firm. Their education centre (itself a tribute to the level of revenue they devote to employee development) at St Charles, Illinois, has a 'Culture Centre' which helps every student and thus in time every partner to take personal ownership of these values. One of the values is 'stewardship', which places a duty on each generation of partners to reverence their inheritance, and to ensure that they pass on to the next generation an improved firm. In business, ethics and integrity are not only good for the soul, they also make cold, hard, good business sense.

Arthur Andersen translate these ethics into a quality statement. 'We are driven by a model of service that includes three key components: added value; building long-term, mutually beneficial relationships; and meeting and exceeding clients' needs and expectations. For us, quality service is nothing short of continuously understanding, accepting, meeting and exceeding clients' needs and expectations.' That is a pretty good definition of TCI.

The message for other organisations is that they have been extraordinarily successful in carrying out their mission. They have highly involved leaders, processes for continuously improving quality, probably the best trained people, ongoing positive recognition from clients and other observers, and the strongest financial position in their industry. They are a model for all consultants.

15. EDUCATION

'The problem we face is primarily a cultural one. The solution must lie in effecting change through the most important source of cultural attitude: education.' *Anthony Tennant, Chairman of Guinness, 1991*

'Perhaps the best book I didn't write was called *Management Ignorance* – there's always so much more around of that than knowledge.' *Peter Drucker, 1992*

'The cost of ignorance vastly exceeds the price of education; that is as equally true for the individual, the business and the nation.' *Anonymous*

The standards of education have become a never-ending talking point in most countries and education is a key priority for governments. With all the discussion, which after all has gone on for years, one might expect that we would get more of it and that it would be better. Unfortunately the educational profession suffers from many of the monopolistic and introverted problems discussed in the previous chapter. In the context of national survival in the competitive world and quality (which is an essential element of that survival) our educational system is failing. The subject is worthy of several books (some of which have already been written) so this short chapter can only touch briefly on three issues – namely, the part general education should play in equipping the next generation for industry and commerce; the role of the business schools; and the applicability of the quality revolution to the process of education. In the main these issues will be viewed from a British standpoint but many of the arguments apply equally to other countries.

The derisory attitude to industry and commerce adopted by the great British public (with the possible exception of those working in them) is baffling. The title 'engineer' carries no status in Britain comparable to that in Germany and Scandinavia; indeed, 'engineer' is more likely to be linked with the gas fitter or the TV repairman. The term 'salesman' conjures up a vision of a 'commercial traveller' in a sleazy hotel. For a short time the computer salesman had high status, presumably because it was assumed that he had to be incredibly clever and earned a lot of money, but the advent of the PC sold over the counter has returned them to limbo. For many in British society the phrase 'in trade' is still applied as an expression of contempt. There is little realisation that industry, commerce and these contemptible trades represent the prime source of wealth for the nation as a whole.

Another aspect of British culture is the worship of the amateur and, in contrast, the feeling that it is somehow vulgar to be professional and successful. This applies equally to sport, politics and business. Initial success may be patriotically acclaimed but everyone is delighted when the hero is shown to have 'feet of clay' and is brought down to size. To mix the metaphors, nobody must be allowed to 'get too big for their boots'. The British have an inherent dislike of precocious foreigners and are quietly proud of their national reputation for reserve and understatement. A dignified modesty is the mark of the English gentleman. To paraphrase a very untypical Englishman, Winston Churchill, the British in many respects 'have much to be modest about'.

The educational system has played and continues to play a large part in creating these cultural attitudes. Anthony Tennant, a leading industrialist, explained it this way in an article in *The Director* magazine: 'The Victorian public schools excluded science from their curricula. And the public schools were themselves the prototype for the 1902 Education Act. The strong sense of antipathy to practical subjects prevalent in public schools was therefore transferred to the state system and the universities.' He continues: 'But Britain's anti-business culture runs deeper, right down to the basic attitudes being inculcated into children, most of whom leave school at 16.... The tendency to confine schoolchildren to taking only three A-Levels creates a narrow focus and allows no scope for the development of communication skills and knowledge of technical application. The result is that employers frequently recruit people who have excellent academic records but no experience of how to apply what they have learned.'

This education system is in marked contrast to other European and Japanese approaches. Science and practical technical education have a much higher priority on their curricula. As a result they produce graduates who enter industry with a high literacy rate in computing and other practical technologies. The Japanese system is the most industry-orientated though it is heavily rote-based and stressful, a fact that is concerning many in Japan. The priority the Japanese give to education, both in the general system and within industry, is to be admired and copied but the methods used are not a model for Western nations.

British education has also been influenced by another factor which stems from the educational revolution that started in the sixties. The massive increase in education funding to meet the post-war baby boom vastly expanded the number of teachers and teacher training colleges. Influenced by the prevailing left-wing thought the training colleges sought to move away from traditional training methods. There was certainly a too heavy reliance on rote-based methods in traditional schooling and it was also arguable that education was overly influenced by middle-class values. However, this revolution, which was meant to introduce a more equal and fair system, swung the pendulum far too far and in some elements was demonstrably silly. Competition was considered unfair to the under-achievers so it was removed. The curricula, examinations and general testing of children was almost eliminated and even competitive sports were discouraged.

These concerns have led the British Government to initiate a series of reforms to the educational system which are as radical as those in the National Health Service. There are major changes in the curricula providing a more practical slant though it could be argued that it has not gone far enough. Testing and evaluation of children not only returns but school performance will be measured on a comparative basis. This is allied to greater parental choice of school with money following the pupil and greater parental involvement in the management of schools. Other reforms put greater emphasis on technical colleges and polytechnics. There are many other facets to the reforms but they are all designed to fit the next generation with a more practical education.

In 1991, President Bush launched a new education strategy entitled 'America 2000' which has similarities to the British reforms. America 2000 is composed of four initiatives that will be pursued simultaneously:

1. Develop better and more accountable schools. A fifteen-point strategy is designed to provide the knowledge and skills students will need to live and work successfully.
2. Create a new generation of American schools. For tomorrow's students, new schools are to be 'invented' to meet the demands of the 21st century. The R & D teams who are to design these new schools consist of members drawn from industrial corporations, universities, think tanks, school innovators and others. They are to be designed for the pursuit of excellence.
3. Create a nation of students. This initiative is aimed to encourage

Americans to continue learning throughout their lives. The Secretaries of Labour and Education will spearhead a public-private partnership to develop voluntary standards for all industries.
4. Create communities where learning can happen. This is aimed to attack the counter-productive influences (drugs and violence) on learning that exist in the communities. Communities will be urged to create local environments conducive to learning.

The US deputy secretary of education, David Kearns, summed up America 2000 by saying: 'Until now most Americans have only read about revolutions in history books. Now everyone has the opportunity to be a part of one.'

Curriculum has been mentioned several times in this chapter but what should children be learning at school to compete in the tougher world? *Fortune* magazine discussed this issue with experts and assembled a list of ten rudiments of a quality education. They said that to prosper in the years ahead, students should, at a minimum, have the following upon graduation from school:

- An ability to communicate effectively, orally and in writing.
- A thorough grounding in literature and the social sciences, especially history and geography.
- An understanding of the principles of higher mathematics, including the ability to apply those principles to daily life.
- Knowledge of the physical sciences, including how those disciplines relate to the environment.
- Mastery of at least one foreign language and culture.
- Thorough familiarity with computers and other technologies to retrieve and use information easily.
- An appreciation of the fine arts.
- A genuine understanding of how government and the economy work.
- Concern for physical health.
- Above all else, the ability to identify problems and work creatively toward solutions.

This is a strong curriculum which at present is matched by too few schools.

Universities and business schools have an essential part to play in the final development of the student to take his part in the new management culture. In that context it is disappointing to note the very low priority given to quality management in higher education. Quality will certainly be included in the curricula of business courses but usually as a subfunction of a business. Again the main concentration is on quality assurance and control rather than the much wider scope of quality management. There are some notable exceptions in both America and the UK. Manchester University (UMIST) has taken a major lead in promoting quality management in the UK and there are chairs of quality management at two other universities.

Apart from quality there has also been strong criticism of the business schools for their slow reaction to changing techniques in industry and service organisations. *The Times* of London on September 23, 1991, in an article by Michael Gyrett, commented: 'Although business schools have enjoyed an unprecedented demand for their services, they often lag behind their customers in practising what they preach. Not until the 1980s did it dawn on many of them that the organisations they advised were more international in outlook and culture than they were. Now they are worried that business education is failing to keep up in terms of product quality and customer service.' Tom Cannon, the Director of the Manchester Business School, says: 'At the prices we charge, companies are entitled to standards of presentation and facilities that, at the very least, match those of independent consultancies and tuition which is not wedded to old-fashioned concepts of university learning.'

The standard of MBA courses is another area of concern which is leading to a fundamental re-design of MBA programmes at business schools in both the UK and the USA. A survey of British companies for the Economist Intelligence Unit's *Which MBA* guide showed that 35 per cent thought that MBA programmes were largely irrelevant and are wrongly designed. Many considered that there was a problem of linking academic theory with practical learning.

Industry and commerce are quick to criticise the education system and the business schools but their own record leaves much to be desired. Very few if any other organisations in the service sector could match Arthur Andersen's investment of 10 per cent of their revenue on educating and training their people. All the companies that have achieved world-class status through the quality revolution emphasise the importance of education to the achievement and have each substantially increased their investment. Unfortunately the majority fall far short of the barest minimum. Figure 14 illustrates diagrams from a report entitled 'Learning Pays', presented by Sir Christopher Ball, and illustrates the effect of these divergent attitudes to education and training.

Finally, to what extent have the educational institutions used TQM to assist their management? Sadly very little; in fact, most wouldn't know what one was talking about if the issue was raised.

LEARNING PAYS

This is the title of an important interim report by Sir Christopher Ball for the RSA, which highlights the importance of training. Amongst many interesting insights are the two diagrams:

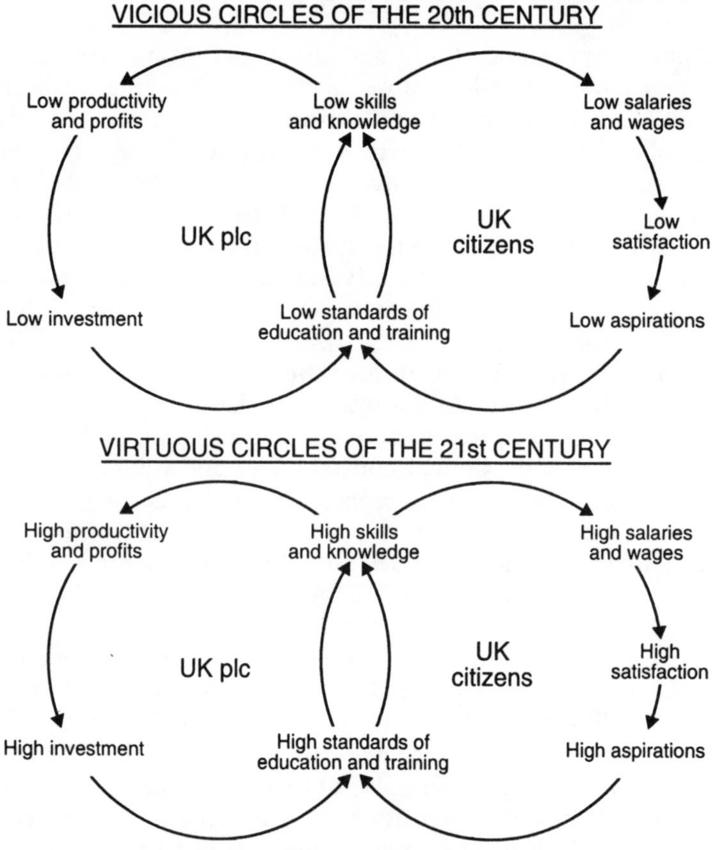

VICIOUS CIRCLES OF THE 20th CENTURY

Low productivity and profits   Low skills and knowledge   Low salaries and wages

UK plc   UK citizens   Low satisfaction

Low investment   Low standards of education and training   Low aspirations

VIRTUOUS CIRCLES OF THE 21st CENTURY

High productivity and profits   High skills and knowledge   High salaries and wages

UK plc   UK citizens   High satisfaction

High investment   High standards of education and training   High aspirations

Figure 14. Attitudes to education and training

The 'we are different' syndrome would echo down most school corridors – 'You cannot manage schools like industry; they are filled with children.' There have been a number of experiments recorded in the USA, usually in small schools and driven by one individual's enthusiasm. Perhaps the most notable experiment in Europe is the implementation of a TQM process in Belgium. The University of Antwerp are facilitating the TQM process in a number of Belgian schools with considerable success. The author has been disappointed that some of the best universities and business colleges in terms of teaching TQM do not actually implement it throughout their own organisations. Is this another case of those who can, do, and those who can't, teach?

15. HOTEL AND CATERING

'There was no room at the Inn.' *New Testament.*

'Why do the British hate their customers?' *Philip Sadler, Vice President, Ashridge Management College*

'Soup is off, luv.' *Peter Sellers.*

'There is no extra charge for the fly, sir.' *Anonymous waiter.*

Despite all the jokes directed at them the hotel and catering industries have probably made more progress in quality than any other single sector of the service industries in recent times. Many hotels and restaurants made quality their main differentiation with their competition for most of this century, but they were exceptions. Probably the first hotel chain to implement what we now call total quality management was the Sheraton Hotels group back in the middle seventies. They were part of the ITT empire and they were therefore influenced by Philip Crosby, then at ITT. Nevertheless, they were pioneers and have generally maintained their commitment to quality. Now a substantial proportion of the industry is familiar with the concepts of quality management. They have to be; the competition is fierce with the vast choice of restaurants and hotels in most cities.

In comparative terms perhaps the most dramatic change can be seen in the UK. The British have long had a bad reputation for service and the standard of catering and hotels. Indeed, British food has been the subject of international jokes (in the British view fostered by the French) for decades. Some of this reputation lingers but most objective observers would agree that this opinion is outdated, with the exception of fast food outlets. This is surprising because customer care in other aspects or sectors of British service is way behind the best standards in the USA or Europe. Years of empire seemed to create an attitude that the concept of service was beneath them. Partly because the British accepted bad service and rarely complained, service industries were organisation rather than customer-driven. 'Never admit the company is at fault – it could create a precedent' seemed to be the prevalent attitude and in any case a complaining customer is 'just being difficult'. But hotels and many restaurants are subject to international rather than just indigenous competition. Whatever the reason, the British hotel and catering industry has reacted positively to that competition. Big names in the field such as Forte, Grand Metropolitan and Gardner Merchant are world leaders.

Hotels and restaurants have always been measured by outside organisations. A variety of 'good food' and hotel guides are published every year and regular travellers consult them assiduously. Searching for two or even three-star restaurants and 'starred' or 'crowned' hotels is a regular pastime for business and leisure travellers. In the case of hotels many travellers are disappointed, mainly because they do not understand the basis of rating. The number of stars or crowns accorded to hotels has nothing to do with the quality standards of the specific hotel. It is only an indication of the *facilities* available such as restaurants, swimming pools, etc. The major guidebooks that award 'stars' to restaurants are based on assessments (some are subjective) and are therefore a guide to the quality of food and service. The leading 'great food' guides have a range of zero to three as their standard. Readers might be interested to know that the city with the highest number of three-star restaurants in the world is not Paris but Brussels. But to the surprise of many there are a substantial number of 'starred' restaurants in the UK.

The quality drive in Britain is not confined to the giant groups. The author makes it a practice to write to the chief executive of any hotel or chain of hotels when he has had bad service. More often he is in a position to tell them that it is their system or lack of training that is at fault rather than individuals. However, he also writes to the chief executive whenever he receives exceptionally good service. Usually it is a matter of congratulating management on their commitment to quality and asking them to commend their staff for their efforts. It is interesting that the number of small groups or individual hotels have figured highly in the appreciative letters. In other words, the quality issue has been taken seriously across the whole market sector.

The first hotel to be certified to BS 5750 was actually a small hotel in a minor industrial town in north-west England. The Avant Hotel in Oldham led the way, followed by giant groups such as Forte and the marketing group Best Western. Tony Buxton, Manager of the Avant Hotel, explains that there is a master manual of standards which is broken down into sections for every department or process in the hotel's operations. For instance, there is a 25-item checklist for each room which is completed every day by the maid. On top of typical duties this includes seeing if light bulbs and all electrical gadgets are operational. An example of the standards set for the Front Desk is illustrated in Figure 15. There is nothing unusual about the standards but they are clearly communicated to the staff and displayed in relevant areas.

Front Desk
Guest Arrival/Check-In Procedure

1. Each guest must be acknowledged immediately upon arrival at Front Desk and served on a first-come first-served basis.

2. All registration transactions must include:
    (a) A welcoming smile.
    (b) Eye-to-eye contact.
    (c) Response to guest arrival, e.g. 'Good morning', 'Good after noon'.
    (d) The use of the guest's name at least once.
    (e) Confirmation of the room type and length of stay.
    (f) Confirmation of method of payment and offer of express checkout, if applicable.
    (g) Handing over of key and key-card with rate clearly shown and directions to room.
    (h) No room number should be mentioned for security reasons.
    (i) Offer of assistance with baggage.
    (j) An appropriate conversation close, e.g. 'I hope you will enjoy your stay'.

3. Guest registration should be an unbroken sequence. Should an unavoidable interruption occur, an apology must be offered to the guest.

4. Every effort must be made to accommodate individual guests immediately. A guest with a confirmed reservation should not be required to wait if his/her arrival is after checkout time. If this is the case, then the guest must:
    (a) Be given an apology and, if feasible, be offered coffee, tea or a drink.
    (b) Be informed of the time when his/her room will be ready.
    (c) Be offered storage facility for luggage.
    (d) Never be sent to a room which is not ready for letting.

Figure 15. The Avant Hotel's checklist.

Though the star system for hotels does not relate to the quality of service, by implication a 'five-star hotel' is the best of its kind and so each customer expects to receive his or her own idea of quality; in a lesser rated or less expensive establishment, a customer may make allowances for shortcomings in any aspect of the 'total meal experience' and will accept that the establishment is only what it purports to be and may happily return again and again. Since there is no higher rating for a hotel, each customer expects perfect service, food and drink and any lapse in quality is seen as a 'breach of promise' and can result in complaints or, worse still, bad publicity spread by disappointed guests.

A hotel that continuously meets those high standards is the Imperial Hotel (part of the Forte Group) in the British holiday town of Torquay. Lawder Smith, Resident Manager, describes the key to their performance as 'a passion for excellence on the part of all staff, created by involvement at all stages of setting, training to and reviewing standards and, above all, generating feedback from guests to measure quality.' Each area has a clear mission statement that relates to the work of every member of the team, whether they be in the restaurant, the bar, the kitchen or the wash-up. The mission for the Imperial Restaurant illustrates the principle: 'We deliver exceptionally high standards of catering that consistently rise above our guest's expectations.' This short, easy to remember statement is displayed throughout the catering areas and all staff are constantly reminded of it and tested upon it. This is supported by operating standards for each department laid down in the 'standards of performance' manual. This is the basis of training for every recruit and provides a constant reminder to each member of staff of what *is* a high standard. Lawder concludes: 'We can never afford to rest on our laurels, despite 125 years of trading at the top end of the market, since today's five-star standard is tomorrow's four-star standard.'

Each of these examples highlights the importance of training. It certainly differentiates the leaders. However, across the whole industry training is a weak link. Generally, employees receive only a few hours of training, usually from fellow workers who themselves are often uncertain of what the requirements of good performance actually are. Again our examples had clearly defined standards. In the USA it is reported that the industry's average time for orientation training is 59 minutes. A contributory factor is the high turnover rates common to the industry. This discourages training, sustained commitment, long-term planning and the attraction of the best people to the industry.

An interesting example of the extension of a quality process into the 'total' environment is demonstrated by the Boston Park Plaza

Hotel, the largest family-run hotel in the USA. They have established a 'Green Team' of enthusiastic hotel employees to implement an 'Environmental Action Program'. This program is designed to conserve energy and water, reduce waste and eliminate hazardous waste and generally concentrate on a recycling program. Tedd Saunders, a member of the owning family, is the Environmental Program Director and states that the program is 'not only to impact our daily operations, but also to reflect our long-term commitment to the earth'. They have established recycling programs for white paper, steel, cardboard, shipping pallets, aluminium, glass and plastic, and created an employee fund with the proceeds from redeemable bottles and cans. They have eliminated Styrofoam throughout the hotel, and they send linens, blankets and furniture to local veterans' shelters where they are needed and reused. This is TCI in action in its widest sense and is an example for every organisation.

The Park Plaza Environmental Program has achieved such fame that Tedd Saunders has established a separate consultancy to assist other organisations and has published a book on the subject entitled *Green is in the Black*.

Quality is an increasing priority for the general catering industry. It is right to emphasise that even prior to the food processing and food poisoning scares of the eighties quality levels in the handling and production of food were, in the main, of a high standard, but certain areas are still found wanting. New legislation has base standards throughout Europe and the sector has responded positively with relevant and beneficial measures. Concentration of effort is moving back in the supply chain to the food and drink processing industry.

Gardner Merchant, the world's leading contract caterer operating in more countries than any other catering company, is another world-class quality organisation. John Forte, Director of Environmental Services with the company, sums up the challenge for the industry: 'Perhaps more than any other sector, the food and drink industry requires total dedication to quality. Any deviation from the highest standard is immediately noticeable to the consumer. There is often no middle man to filter complaints. Food or drink can literally be thrown back into the face of the vendor or supplier. Without the most rigorous quality controls, those operating in the catering industry may as well go home. Only the most dedicated to health, safety, hygiene and radiant cleanliness will survive in the market.'

PART THREE

Making It Happen

The practical steps on the journey
to total and continuous improvement

16. PROVIDING THE ENVIRONMENT

Executives and senior managers have the crucial role in the creation of an organisation committed to total and continuous improvement. No one else has the authority or control of resources to make it happen. It most certainly will not happen just by desire or by accident. Executives must plan for it to happen and then cause it to happen.

To ensure focus on the issues and actions involved in making it happen, the process can be best viewed as containing three elements (see Figure 16). These elements can be summarised as providing the environment, the process and the support. This chapter will concentrate on the first element – providing the environment – and the next chapters will discuss the other two elements. However, it should be emphasised that no one element stands on its own. Yet too often that is exactly what does happen. To quote John Krappenberger, Director of Quality at TRW Inc., 'We (in the West) have made quality progress, but with a few notable exceptions we haven't made that critical leap towards fully utilising our human resources in the pursuit of quality.' It is the author's contention that a failure to comprehend or to maintain all these elements in balance is a major contributor to the comparative failure of the West in the quality revolution.

Roger Milliken, chief executive officer of Milliken and Company and a quality pioneer, has said that 'only three barriers exist to the quality improvement process: the first is top management; the second is middle management; the third is first line management.'

Milliken is not berating deliberately obstructive managers but underlining the fact that current management practices inhibit the real involvement of the employees in the pursuit of quality. There are many barriers to communication or comprehension between each level of management just as there are barriers between departmental peers at each level. But there are some classic barriers that have been identified by Faith Ralston, a Minneapolis pioneer in the behavioural aspects of TQM (see Figure 17), which create an imple-

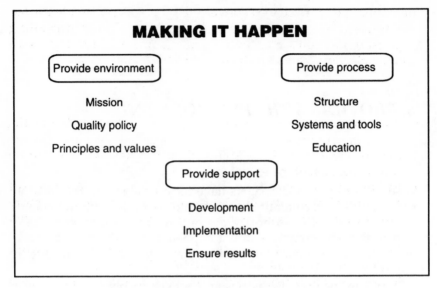

Figure 16. Planning and causing it to happen

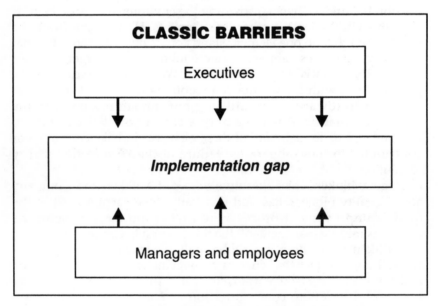

Figure 17. The implementation gap

mentation gap between executive intention and the wholehearted commitment of the managers and employees. In our prevailing organisational culture executives, managers and employees all exhibit behaviour patterns which could be summarised as follows:

Executives

- Will often make decisions with little or no knowledge of the implication of those decisions on the systems or people who have to implement them. In TCI terms they may have a vision but no comprehension of the roadmap.
- Fail to communicate effectively. They rarely seek a wide range of operational opinions before making decisions and even more rarely explain the reasons for those decisions to those charged with implementation.
- Work as individuals and not as teams. They call for teamwork throughout the organisation but exclude themselves.
- Rarely act as they talk. They exhort the workforce to 'put quality first' and then continually make decisions which blatantly compromise quality.
- Fail to establish measurable criteria for other than short-term financial or people measurement.
- Fail to lead or create organisational excitement. They are all too often remote from their organisations.

Managers

- Feel stressed or overstretched in matching executive decree to ability to implement.
- Lack enthusiasm for change; they have been caught before.
- Fail to collaborate or practise teamwork with their peers.
- Not only fail to communicate effectively but create a 'purposeful fog' which inhibits communication.
- Ape executives in actions, lack of measurement and failure to lead.

Employees

- Are left in the dark. They are the victims of the mushroom management joke.
- They feel that they are at the bottom of the pit with no one left to hit.
- They feel scepticism and mistrust.
- They feel unheard and unappreciated.
- As a result they are unable to release their potential.

This may be a jaundiced view of behaviour in the majority of organisations. Yet the author can confirm from his own experience in dozens of organisational assessments that these are typical patterns. Perhaps more significantly the evidence is drawn from organisations numbered amongst the best. After all, they are the companies who are most likely to invest in assessing their current position with an intention to improve.

These behaviour patterns are based on perceptions or beliefs which are in themselves assumptions about what is true. The trouble with organisational behaviour is that perceptions quickly become facts, because people tend to act within the framework of their perceptions. As Faith Ralston argues, if we are to bridge the implementation gap we need to change these perceptions by finding new ways of managing, working and thinking (see Figure 18). We must adopt a dramatically different set of principles and values that will change the beliefs of managers and employees. Executives should start by assessing their own organisation and considering whether their current culture provides an environment conducive to TCI.

The old perceptions and beliefs are rooted in the history of organisational growth. To some extent traditional management practices

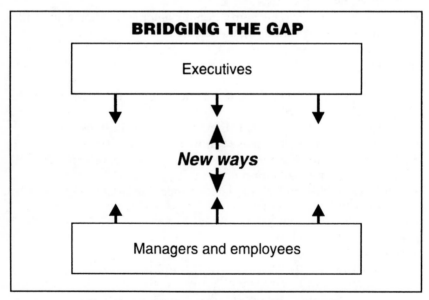

Figure 18. Finding new ways of managing

served industry well for a long period but they are now being challenged by a series of social revolutions which are rendering them obsolete. Comprehension of these historical roots and of the new social pressures are essential prerequisites for the development of new principles and values which will provide the environment for TCI.

Earlier chapters noted the effect of 'Taylorism' on the growth of traditional management practices. An American consultant, Robert F. Lynch, has perceptively summed up this era by the principles of control, command and compliance which he said were symbolised by the management styles of Henry Ford, George Patton and first-grade teachers everywhere. He described them as 'ghosts of management past who embody those traditional principles'.

Ford, working closely with Taylor, introduced the assembly line. 'Jobs were designed so that each worker had one highly repetitive task to accomplish.... Jobs that required many skills were replaced by narrowly defined jobs in which supervisors made all the decisions.' The worker didn't have to think – indeed it was dangerous to allow him to do so: he just had to be controlled. Lynch goes on to say that 'the control principle results in walls being constructed between thinkers and doers and between departments' [the fortress mentality described in *Global Quality - The New Management Culture*]. The vertical nature of the organisation is the most prominent feature. When problems exist between departments, the problem-solving approach is to tell the boss, who informs his or her boss... the reality of the horizontal work flow has been ignored... so that managers can retain an artificial sense of control.'

George Patton epitomised the principle of command management in which the leader is perceived as the fount of all wisdom. To quote Lynch: 'A generation of managers grew up believing that the way to win was to clearly give direct orders, demand complete loyalty, and punish any offenders.... The legacy of command permeates most organisations today and snuffs out commitment, creativity and spirit.' Though Lynch goes on to argue that the command principle was right for Patton's time and task, a European could argue that even then it depended on the purpose for which the command principle was utilised. After all, the above is also an accurate description of Adolf Hitler's management style.

Robert Lynch's description of the compliance principle comes ever closer to the environment found in the majority of today's organisations. 'Doing things the way they have always been done dominates. The compliance principle is operating when people are expected to do what they are told, do it the proven way, and defer to rank even when a better idea might exist. The formal and informal systems reward people for waiting to be told what to do and maintaining the status quo. If an employee tries something different and it doesn't work, he or she is sure to be punished.' He concludes that the entire educational system is designed to teach people to do things the one right way as defined by the authority figure: 'Our first-grade teachers prepared us to work for Patton.'

These traditional principles of control, command and compliance must be replaced by new principles based on commitment, consensus and creativity. We shall return to discuss new principles and values later but first let's examine the social revolutions which are challenging this cosy triumvirate. Perhaps above all they are attacking the principle of compliance without which control and command are unworkable.

Organisations do not grow or operate in a vacuum. There are a host of external influences (even occasionally the customer!) which help determine the perceptions and beliefs that make up the culture of an organisation. Principles and values designed to replace amorphous perceptions must take into account five distinct but linked revolutions which are impacting the nature of business, the structure of organisations and the behaviour and attitudes of managers and workers alike. Figure 19 represents these five revolutions as linked circles highlighting the interaction between each and all, centred around the principles and values of organisational culture. Volumes could be written (and have been) about each of the revolutions but a short explanation will have to suffice for the purpose of this chapter.

The demographic revolution

Substantial changes are taking place in the composition of populations across the world. These changes are bound to affect both the nature of work and the migration of industry types across continents. Though the revolution differs from nation to nation it can be broadly summarised as a major reduction in birth rates in the advanced or the wealthiest nations. Falling infant mortality rates in the poorer nations and rapidly improving longevity in the wealthier nations are changing the population numbers and balance between young and old. In Britain, for example, 1995 will see half the number of school leavers that were experienced in 1985.

Economic pressure at home in the poorer nations and the advent of relatively cheap or easy travel have created new migratory patterns. The recent political changes in Eastern Europe are likely to promote more major population migrations. Increasingly the richer nations are resorting to tougher immigration controls. However, if

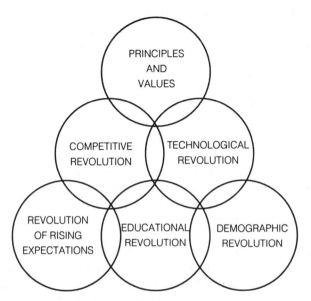

Figure 19. The five revolutions

the people do not migrate many industries, particularly but not exclusively manufacturing industry, will migrate to join the people or, in the language of business, 'cheaper labour'.

All these movements are well advanced and are rapidly changing the service/industry mix in the richer nations. They will also profoundly affect the employment of women and the nature of retirement. Remember the changes in employment patterns caused by the reduction of the number of men of working age during the two world wars.

The competitive revolution

A pervading influence throughout this book and the subject of the author's earlier book, *Global Quality – The New Management Culture*, has been the impact of the Japanese-led quality revolution. This revolution is clearly influencing the thinking of managers in both manufacturing and service industries. But this revolution is inextricably intertwined with a similar revolution often referred to as the 'market-led economy or society'. Seen in that light the competitive revolution is clearly having a massive influence on society as a whole. Whole nations are under its influence and it clearly embraces service sectors such as healthcare and government agencies. The worldwide competitive revolution is the stimulant for much of the change that abounds and not least the revolution of rising expectations.

The technological revolution

The pace of technological change this century has been breathtaking and it is still accelerating. As we absorb each change we ourselves are changed and it becomes difficult to visualise our lives before the change came about. Try explaining to grandchildren what the world was like before cars, planes, telephones, television and computers. Yet none of them existed at the start of the Industrial Revolution or even in the lifetime of some of us now. Equally it is difficult to envisage the change in our lives that will come about through the application of technological change already in the pipeline, let alone others only at the conceptual stage. We have watched wide-eyed the technology paraded in the Gulf War and witnessed the collapse of a coup and the resultant demise of Communism largely brought about by the power of satellite communications. (The latter is an interesting example of the effect of relaxing compliance on a command and control structure.) In a sense the technological revolution is largely a communications revolution. This aspect of technology will have a dominant impact on future organisations.

It is already feasible for a substantial proportion of business processes to be carried out by independently mobile individuals without ever needing to go near a central office. At home or in a car the individual can now command information and maintain communication with only a few devices: a video telephone, linked to an answerphone, a facsimile printer and a computer in turn linked to a network of other computers all communicating through satellites. Miniaturisation will soon make all of these devices combined no larger than a conventional briefcase. This mobility is rapidly becoming economically justifiable without even considering the reduction of expensive office space. It does not require a great deal of imagination to see the implications of this change on the current organisation.

Within a few years this change will not be decided on the available technology or cost but on principles and values. Will management be prepared to relinquish the traditional command and control practices implicit in this level of independent operation?

The educational revolution

We saw earlier that the needs of industry as discerned by Henry Ford in the control ethic were the reduction of individual skills in the workforce. The technological revolution and the increasing complexity of work processes have now put this trend in reverse. Increasingly the robotic tasks of the early workers have been taken over by machines. But the control of those machines and processes has required an increasingly skilled and thinking workforce of both management and workers.

Quite apart from the needs of industry, social changes have provided ever widening educational opportunities for all levels of society. Educated workers are less likely to remain compliant to the same extent. (It is an interesting conjecture whether the rise of dissidents which led to the collapse of a compliant Communism was the result of the general rise in education in the USSR or of the very high levels of education required of scientists and technologists in the furtherance of technology.)

Education stimulates thought and provokes a challenging attitude to many traditional management practices. This is a key consideration in the evolution of a TCI culture. This has to be married to the clear need in industry and commerce for an increasingly better educated and multi-skilled workforce. An increasingly used axiom is worth repeating: it would be more profitable to evaluate the cost of ignorance rather than the cost of education.

The requirement for a more highly educated workforce is compounded by the facts of the demographic revolution. The sophisticated economies cannot long sustain the awful wastage of people resource which for one reason or another results from their respective national educational systems. Education and the development of all the population is rapidly becoming a priority of survival. Education has wider horizons than meeting the needs of industry and commerce, but equally it cannot ignore them.

Another aspect of the educational revolution will require changes in management thinking in a similar area highlighted by the demographic revolution. In Britain close to fifty per cent of university graduates are women. Some forty per cent of those desperately-needed educated resources are lost to industry and commerce within seven years. The provision of crèches is a very minor application of the new managerial practices demanded to manage this aspect of tomorrow's industry. Women share in the revolution of expectations.

The burning of bra's was only a bizarre initial symptom of this particular change. Throughout the world, however sophisticated the economy, command and control is still dominated by male chauvinism, albeit often unconscious. The whole attitude can be summed up in the apocryphal phrase, 'It is very unfair to treat women as equals; it only confuses them.'

The revolution of rising expectations

The revolution of rising expectations is not confined to the Third World. It take many forms but it is present in almost all societies. With some it may be confined to lifting their heads above mere survival; with others it will be expressed in terms of quality of life or perhaps a more focused desire to determine their individual destinies. This may prove to be the most powerful of all the revolutions in modifying the structure and managerial principles of future organisations in the sophisticated economies.

The author well remembers his first experience of this revolution in practice back in the middle seventies. He was then employed by one of the world's leading corporations. Aspiring and company-recognised potential for future high-level general management posts were required to prove their worth in the far-flung posts of empire. In American terms this might involve running the UK. In British terms it would involve managing Scotland, Ireland or the Northern Region of England. The potential leaders would disappear to their respective colonial outposts of the corporate empire. The best quickly proved themselves and were invited back to substantial promotions on the corporate ladder. But in the interim something had changed. They and their families had discovered the quality of life. Land, paddocks and minimal commuting had established a new set of personal values. 'Why on earth do I need to go through all the stresses of central corporate or big city life when I have everything here I need for the good life?'

The corporation may bewail their lack of ambition or their loss of that beloved phrase, 'the killer instinct'. But the corporation was wrong; they had just replaced one ambition with another ambition. And in the author's view it would be a brave or ignorant man who said that the corporation was right and that the individual was wrong.

Increasingly intelligent and ambitious workers and managers will demand a greater say in their business destinies and their quality of life. In Britain there have been cynical comments about the heat in kitchens directed at politicians who have resigned for the ostensible reason 'to spend more time with their families'. Well pressure cooking may have been a contributory factor in their decision but it could be wiser for the future of our organisational practices to take their explanations at face value. Obvious technical talent and leadership potential cannot be squandered on the altar of corporate procedures rooted in traditional practices. Successful organisations will be those who master all the implications of the revolution of rising expectations. Link this train of thinking with the individual mobility provided by the technological revolution and a new 'free form' organisational structure will soon replace the typical authoritarian pyramid.

Everything that has gone before in this chapter should make it clear that the development of a mission or purpose statement and a set of supporting principles and values will not of themselves provide the environment for TCI. Management will have to put the principles and values into practice. This may take courage. It could involve a radical change in existing management practices and procedures.

Max Weber, the German social scientist, said as long ago as 1917 that the organisational leader develops organisational excitement by:

- Developing a common purpose for the organisation.
- Creating value-related opportunities within a large framework of the organisation's goals.
- Enabling employees to feel more in control of their individual and collective destinies.

This statement may appear simple on the surface but its practical application is by no means easy. It indicates that cultural change must be related to the goals of the business. These are sometimes referred to as the soft and hard issues of managerial strategy. But they are issues, not alternative options. They emphasise that only new principles that maximise the human potential will provide the ultimate business goals. We have to link people and their new-found aspirations to technology in ways that optimise the potential of both. Figure 20 indicates the areas for management attention if they are to put the principles into action.

Leaders need to develop a purpose and supporting principles and values which can be shared by all employees of the organisation, management and workers alike. This should form the basis of the desired organisational culture. These new principles must be communicated in such a way that ownership of the principles is transferred to everyone. This is most usually accomplished by education which encourages employees to identify the contradictions to those practices in their current culture. But this will not be enough to convert employee attitudes into improved performance to the levels required to sustain competitive advantage.

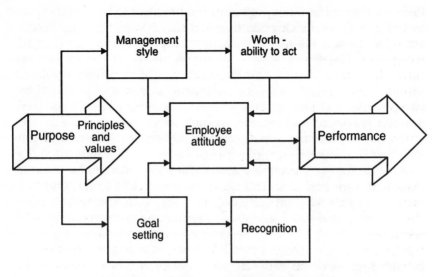

Figure 20. Putting principles into action

Executives themselves must also take ownership of the new principles to the extent that they examine and amend all the traditional procedures and practices which determine employee attitudes. All too often management enthusiastically embrace the new principles and values which they have developed and then totally ignore the implications on their own behaviour. They must turn their attention to four main areas described below if they are to provide the true environment for total and continuous improvement.

Management style

The traditional style of control and command must be replaced by a participatory and listening style, a style based on leadership rather than management. As Philip Crosby has said, the role of managers is to *help* people achieve improved performance rather than just order improvement: seek their collaboration rather than insisting on blind compliance.

Worth or ability to act

A confident and proud workforce will add a colossal value or worth to the overall performance of an organisation. Employee confidence and self-esteem as part of a team leads to pride in their work and in their company. Management recognition of the worth of employees as individuals is the determining factor in developing this attitude amongst employees. (This need is not to be confused with peer recognition, discussed later.) Deep down a sense of personal worth comes from the realisation that individuals can influence the organisation. This level of influence will vary from one to another. The passive personalities will be delighted that from time to time their opinion is sought and listened to by leaders. Active personalities will want to be leaders and for them delight will come from the ability to act on their own judgement.

All the above is probably readily acceptable to most modern managers in a philosophical mood. But therein lies the crunch – turning acceptable philosophies into actual practice. In an earlier chapter the point was made that senior management control all the resources. Individual ability to act is most often related to the use of resource. Releasing the potential of the workforce does depend on a management decision to share some control of the resources of the organisation. Every manager can find a thousand reasons why releasing the control of resources would be a dangerous course for the organisation. It sounds like soft management and we all know what happens when you allow laxity of expense control in a salesforce.

Releasing the control of resources has an element of risk. Without other complementary actions to ensure responsibility it could lead to anarchy and a total loss of direction towards the purpose. A dichotomy faces the future manager: 'If I release control of resources the business goes down the tubes; if I don't I will never release the potential of people to grow the business in the new competitive world.' Weak managers avoid risk; strong managers learn to minimise risk. Management need to change direction and find an answer to the conundrum of the five revolutions (see Figure 19).

This issue goes to the heart of the new management culture. There are no easy answers. Just as the deficiencies of the control ethic are now clear for all to see we can also find examples of the 'participatory' approach leading to a loss of focused direction. To replace control with 'wishy-washy' management is not the answer. Management must learn to advance in a balanced approach to the total environment. The author believes that the answer will come from the controlled release of resources; evolution not revolution. Ideals are part of the vision but their application in practice can produce nebulous results, if only because of the ingrained habits of traditional reaction on the part of both management and people.

Goal setting

This is another part of the balanced equation. Deming has reiterated that management is obsessed with the numerate measurement of people. This is a natural corollary to the vertical division of organisations for control purposes. Management by objectives, individual payment by results, piece-work incentives and many appraisal systems only reinforce the fortress mentality. They actively discourage collaboration between departments and teamwork. The organisation seeking to provide a new environment will examine all these prevailing practices in the light of the new principles and values. It is a comparative evaluation which should lead to new practices. The comparator is: to what extent do our methods of reward and goal setting actively promote mutual trust and collaboration? Too many present practices promote only anxiety and fear. Operational goal setting itself should be a mutual and collaborative exercise unified around the common purpose.

Recognition

Management will demonstrate its recognition of individual contribution by its commitment to change traditional practices and procedures. However, it should also encourage mutual respect of each other by the whole workforce. Peer recognition is a powerful motivator which provides self-esteem and confidence. Corporate values use phrases such as 'we will treat each other with dignity and respect'. It is a sad commentary on modern society that simple courtesy is no longer the norm. Where it exists in an organisation it is immediately obvious. The employees are all smiling and 'thank you' seems the most common phrase on the lips of management and people. Management can 'kick start' the process of mutual recognition by introducing formal recognition systems based on the concepts of peer recognition.

Practical examples

The following examples of a mission and supporting principles and values are reproduced by kind permission of the St Helier National Health Service Trust. This is a major unit of four hospitals in the Merton and Sutton district of the South-West Thames Region of the National Health Service in southern England.

Together with the Trust's definition of quality and the quality policy they represent a fundamental reassessment of the role of the hospitals in the community.

Of course the Trust are well aware that the mere statement of principles and values is not in itself sufficient to ensure that a new environment will result. They have implemented a major educational initiative to include every employee from the specialist consultant surgeon to the hospital porter. The syllabus includes thorough discussion of the principles and the changes they indicate as well as providing competence in the practical use of quality management tools.

1
Mission

The purpose of the St Helier NHS Trust is to respond to individual patient needs.

* We will achieve this by offering a comprehensive range of specialised health care services.

* We will continuously improve the quality of our services.

* We will be a progressive employer by enabling staff to realise their full potential.

* We will provide a high level of medical and professional education.

* We will grow by providing quality services to an increasing number of patients.

2
Quality Definition

Pleasing our patients, clients and colleagues by continuously meeting and improving upon agreed requirements.

3
Quality Policy

* We will identify and respond to the health needs of each of our patients and strive to exceed their expectations of us.

* We recognise that the special nature of health care requires each individual to carry out their duties conscientiously and without delay.

* We will further improve our service by continuous review and critical evaluation of our work.

* We will fully understand the requirements of our jobs and will conform to them and our professional requirements at all times.

4
Principles and Values

We are in partnership with our patients, their doctors and Health Authorities dedicated to the relief of ill health and promotion of improved wellbeing for our patients. The word 'patient' is a generic term to include all consumers of health care, for example clients, users, residents, etc.

* We will treat all our patients with dignity, courtesy and respect.

* We recognise that each person is a unique individual whose needs are physical, emotional, spiritual and social.

* We will protect the confidentiality of our patients' personal matters at all times.

* We will honour our patients' rights for information, explanation and participation in their care process.

The St Helier NHS Trust is dedicated to the success of its service and recognises that its Mission can only be achieved through people. Therefore:

* We all have a responsibility towards providing a quality service.

* We will each commit ourselves to continuous self-development.

* We will recognise individuals for their contribution.

* We will communicate with each other in an open and frank manner.

* We recognise that all our people want to do a good job and need to know exactly what is expected of them.

The management board of The St Helier Trust is committed to continuous improvement and leadership by:

* Defining the Mission, Quality Policy, Principles and Values of the Trust.

* Ensuring that there is continuous education and self-improvement for everyone.

* Removing all the barriers that prevent improvement and open communication being achieved.

* Creating an environment that will enable our staff to make their maximum contribution to the care of our patients.

* Ensuring that all their actions uphold the Principles and Values of the Trust

---

There are many ways to express the purpose and principles and values of the organisation. Each organisation must find its own expression which the employees can share. Too often the release of a new company video or publication of principles is greeted derisively by employees with comments such as 'I wonder where that is – it would be a nice company to work for!' The publication of principles must be supported by action and be capable of communication to the workforce. A good example is that developed by Jamie Houghton, Chairman of the board of Corning Glass Ware.

A Total Quality Company is one...

...where the customer means more than just to whom we sell.

...whose requirements are understood and met so we can profitably conduct business.

...whose products are of such unquestioned Quality that they can be received without incoming inspection.

...who uses suppliers who know that Quality is more important than price.

...who pursues training and education for every employee that directly translates in doing the job right first time and with supervisors encouraging them to do so.

...where employees run their own areas, solve their own problems, with the supervisors acting as advisers.

...where employees work as a true team, knowing that in the long run it is simply in their mutual best interest.

...where people are trusted and trust each other, where fear of job loss is only real when performance is poor.

...where management pays as much attention to Quality plans and their results as we do today to budgets.

...in which each employee lives Quality as the key value, a value as unquestioned as integrity.

Jamie Houghton, Chairman of the board C.G.W.
Rochester, October 1983

17. PROVIDING THE PROCESS

The organisation can define where it wants to go but it also has to provide the TQM process or the vehicle which will carry everyone on the journey. The executives have defined the purpose of the organisation and the new values which provide the environment for change. They will continue to have a major role, not least in providing the resources and a constancy of purpose in ensuring that the change is taking place. However, it is the role of operational managers to make it happen and to provide the process by which the change will be brought about and maintained.

There are two aspects to the manager's role in taking ownership of the actions needed to make it happen. One is the fundamental change in their own behaviour from their traditional command and control practices. (This will be discussed in the next chapter, 'Supporting the Process'.) The other aspect is developing the systematic elements of the TQM process. These will include the organisational structure, the systems and tools to assist people achieve improvement and the education for everyone in the organisation. (Much of the detail involved here was described in the author's *Global Quality – The New Management Culture* and this chapter will concentrate on the main issues and some of the dangers or risks gleaned from implementation experience.)

Danger – Managers at Work

One principle of the new desired culture is the recognition that the people actually doing the job know best how to do it. This principle is not confined to the relationship between supervisor and worker. As we saw in the last chapter, the barrier starts between executives and operational managers. This is a primary reason for transferring ownership of the process to management. However, there is an immediate danger to be faced from the start. That is that the managers will then react in their traditional manner to executive strategic initiatives. For years the divisive practices of MBO and departmental goal setting have committed them to an 'action this day' approach or the alternative attitudes of apathy and scepticism. Many will translate the executive decision into a personal drive to show that they are going to be the winners or performers in this new initiative. Others will go along with the words but not really change many actions as from their experience they will expect this to be just a passing phase.

Large organisations particularly are a hotbed of individual politics, empire building, competition and implied threat and a general lack of interdepartmental collaboration. Executives should be mindful of these realities and establish a team of managers representing each function or department to plan the process collaboratively from the start. As Abraham Lincoln once said: 'If I had eight hours to fell a tree, I'd spent four hours sharpening the axe.' They need to find a balance between the old British disease of planning forever without action and the American tendency to act without enough thought.

Preparing the plan

If the planning team (often referred to as facilitators) are to break down the traditional fortresses they need to understand the new direction for which they are planning. They, therefore, are the first group to need education and this is generally recognised by quality management consultants. The aim of this education is to ensure that the facilitators will first recognise the need to change, take personal ownership of the need and fully understand the principles of TQM and TCI.

A warning at this stage. For real ownership of the need to change it has to be directly related to the specific organisation. To send the facilitators away to an outside quality management course based on generic theory and broad principles for action is dangerous, however eminent the advice. The author's approach is to use a planning workshop which relates need to the initial organisational assessment and the principles established by the work with the executives. At the completion of a typical four-day workshop the facilitators will have established clear assignments for elements of their *own* plan. These assignments will need to be worked on to finalise detail and design and brought together in a one-day workshop.

A typical example of the contents of a plan to provide the process is that developed by the National Health Service unit mentioned earlier and reproduced here.

Contents
Introduction

1 Mission
2 Quality Definition
3 Quality Policy
4 Principles and Values
5 Quality Education
6 Tools and Systems
7 Structure
8 Quality Management Team Interface
9 Terms of Reference of Quality Management Teams
10 Involvement of Acute Services Management Board
11 Key Process Analysis
12 Measurement of Success

Appendices

1 Management Education
2 Work Group Education
3 Broad timeframe — Education
4 Education resource requirements
5 Input/Output/Process Requirements/Activity Analysis
6 Examples of charting of non-conformance
7 Corrective Action System
8 Shadow Organisation
9 Quality Implementation Group — Task Groups
10 Broad timeframe — TQM process

This is a good example of the elements that need to be considered in developing a plan that will provide the process. Other subjects often included are the role of improvement and innovation groups (these will be discussed in Chapter 19, 'Finding Joy in Work'). But a number of issues lie buried in this list which need special mention in this chapter.

Structure

The departmentalised attitudes and empire-building tendencies of operational management are often in evidence in planning the organisation for quality improvement. They can result in an institutionalised organisation which takes ownership of quality improvement. Another fortress is created and quality is seen as a separate function rather than an integral part of normal business. Unfortunately many consultants in the search for easy to communicate methodologies fall into the same trap with a host of quality improvement teams which tend to view quality as a project.

The planning team have to recognise the distinction between managing change and managing quality. Any organisation they establish should be designed to provide the process for *use* by management and people. This organisation would develop the corrective action *system* but never take responsibility for corrective *action*. Quality and business operations are not divisible. Continuous improvement is the responsibility of everyone in the organisation, not a specialist or elite group. This is a particular area for executive review of the process in action. Quality is simply the way we work.

Tools and systems

A substantial array of tools has been developed for the TQM process. In general they support measurement, analysis and problem-solving and are described in Chapter 23. In providing the process, the planning team must realise that these tools should be available and that they may have to plan for specialist training to provide competence in their use. A substantial number of tools should be explained in the TQM educational process as a basic requirement to support the process. Contrary to the opinions of some Deming enthusiasts, the universal use of statistical process control is not the total answer for continuous improvement. The organisation must make an initial choice of the tools most appropriate to their operations. They can always add to the 'tool kit' as the journey continues. Changes must be introduced at the pace the organisation can digest. Each tool, once mastered and generally applied, will prompt further development. The improvement process will learn from itself.

Measurement and analysis must have a meaningful purpose. Both are tools to communicate objectively with facts about the performance of work processes and should lead to action. In the early stages of improvement (before managers have really learnt to empower people) this usually means communication to management asking for help. Here the TQM process can come up against two barriers to communication that are typical of traditional management attitudes. Both are related to feedback from workers to management. Management likes to operate in the 'good news syndrome'. It generally associates subordinates who bring them problems with negative attitudes: 'Don't keep bringing me problems, bring me solutions.' Even those who bring solutions are sometimes told: 'Stop meddling with things that do not concern you.' Management does not like its sins exposed by bottom-up feedback. Managers at heart do not really understand that their real role in life is to *help* their people. They should actively encourage the objective reporting of problems and see the process as an opportunity to help and improve.

Managers should now believe that they must improve communication with the workforce. However, they too often see it as one-way communication through 'team briefings' or newsletters about how the overall company is performing or to describe some new employee benefits. One employee, asked about the 'new open and frank communication in the organisation', replied: 'We communicate openly about all the trivial things but we never communicate openly about making boxes.' But making boxes was the purpose of their business. Management will readily accept feedback from a control device, but not from a worker. The view seems to be, 'What does he know about it?' Yet continuous feedback is at the heart of continuous improvement. To quote Philip Crosby, 'Management has to learn to give people the permission to get it right first time.' Our present management practices give people permission to get it wrong and, worse still, go on getting it wrong, over and over again. No wonder they lose interest in improvement.

The use of measurement and process analysis tools by workers will aid communication about work: in other words, communication with peers in other groups, with management and with subordinates. To ensure that management really change their behaviour and start to listen, a formal closed-loop corrective action system should be designed at the planning stage; in other words, a corrective action system in which problems are noted, logged, action taken and reported back to the originator. If action cannot be taken or will take time then that must also be fed back. Such systems should provide multi-access from all levels in the organisation and, where possible, designed to take account of existing error logging systems. Many companies have elaborate error logging methods (particularly for field service operators) but rarely have a system to ensure that the root causes of errors are identified and eradicated forever. Workers are left to keep on 'quick fixing' the same old errors.

If recognition, just saying 'thank you', is not a natural part of the culture of the organisation then the facilitators should consider developing a formal peer recognition system. This area has been fully described in *Global Quality – the New Management Culture.*

Education and training

The development of education for every individual in the organisation is a major element in providing the TQM process. Education is the vehicle to accomplish the mind-set change essential for the journey to TCI. It should help everyone to recognise the need to change from their own perspective so that they can take personal ownership of the need. It is also the most powerful method of communicating comprehension of the purpose of the organisation and the supporting principles and values. Merely publishing new values is to little avail. People must have the opportunity to question them and see the present contradictions all around them. That way leads to comprehension and the gradual development of a shared culture or partnership between management and people.

The training aspect is designed to provide competence in the use of the new tools and systems. The natural use of these tools will provide a common language for all in the organisation. The barriers to communication will collapse when all speak the common language of quality and measurement instead of the current babel of executive middle management and worker.

So the purpose of quality education is to involve every employee in the improvement process. This will be achieved by developing a shared culture based on shared values and knowledge. The objectives of quality education are:

- For everyone to work in a different way – in other words, change their traditional behaviour.
- Lay the foundation for continuous improvement in all the activities of the organisation.

In developing an educational plan there are two key factors to ensure effectiveness: timing and concept. An educational process that goes too fast can result in lack of proper comprehension and commitment. Similarly, if it takes too long the process could be blown off course or the participants wait too long before putting the theory into practice with loss of training effect. But the most important factor is that the concept of adult learning is properly understood. Adults learn best by *doing* in their own work environment. Adult learning is about facilitation, not teaching.

Much management training is based on accounting methods of

making things balance – that is, subtracting negative figures from positive figures to give an overall periodic balance and the balance hides the good and the bad (this paragraph was amongst the author's jottings; if it is a direct quote he apologises to the original author).

The basic approach to adult learning should be transitional from learning to action as follows:

THEORY ⟶ PRACTICE ⟶ ACTION

Education and training should be organised in a series of short sessions spaced about one week apart, rather than sending managers and others away on courses of several days far from their workplace. This allows action to take place between each session and aids the transition. The transition for each session should be based on reading a little theory before each session and using a workbook for recording practice and action. The typical approach to each session is illustrated below.

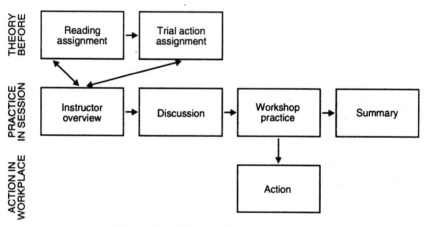

Figure 21. The training process

Figure 21 is a broad description of the concept of management education (a detailed example of material content is included in *Global Quality – The New Management Culture*). A classroom environment with the usual facilities for a cross-functional team of approximately ten managers has been found the ideal environment. Each manager should be supplied with an individual workbook which later becomes a working reference guide. This process should start with the executives and cascade down to the first-line managers or supervisors. The specialists or knowledge workers should also be included at this level of education.

Once the managers of a particular operation have concluded their education and hopefully begun to change their behaviour the next stage can begin. Natural work groups should be trained by their own supervisors. This process should be more directly related to work place action and should be held as near to the area of work as possible. Though individual workbooks are used the sessions should not be in or have a classroom environment. In essence the work group are starting an improvement group which should continue on a regular basis once the basic concepts and methods have been learned.

This educational process will not achieve its objectives unless the whole TQM process is properly supported, and that is the subject of the next chapter.

18. SUPPORTING THE PROCESS

'No lesson seems to be so deeply inculcated by the experience of life as that you never should trust experts. If you believe the doctors, nothing is wholesome: if you believe the theologians, nothing is innocent: if you believe the soldiers, nothing is safe. They all require to have their strong wine diluted by a very large admixture of insipid common sense.'

Lord Salisbury's quotation could have been designed to describe the process of implementing total quality management. An eager management is beset by experts and gurus and often ends up confused. A typical way out of the confusion is to blindly select one of the experts and then forcefully present the new gospel to all and sundry. Few listen and management wonders why TQM is so difficult to implement. Actually the principles of TQM are very simple and are in essence only the application of sound common sense. Unfortunately there is nothing so common in traditional management practices as the lack of common sense.

Intelligent managers, with their experience of business life, will have recognised the need to change. They will conceptually understand the reasons for providing the environment for change, in the sense of establishing a purpose and principles and values for the organisation. They will also understand the need to provide a process for change, in the sense of educating the employees and providing systems and tools for all to use. They may even understand the need to support the process of change, in the sense of changing their behaviour. Too often they do not fully comprehend the *degree* of change needed in their behaviour and *actions*. Despite being wedded to the new objectives management have a tendency to fall back on the tried and proven methods of command and compliance. It is not wholly fair to blame them because they have adopted this behaviour from experience. They are attempting to *control* the implementation of TQM in the same old ways albeit with courtesy and in the spirit of participation. But deep down they have not really understood the level of change demanded of them to achieve a sustained competitive advantage.

TQM does require a profound level of change in the behaviour of management. They will not change the attitudes of employees without changing themselves. Both management and employees must change to unlock their combined potential for the ultimate success of the organisation. Though the change needed is profound

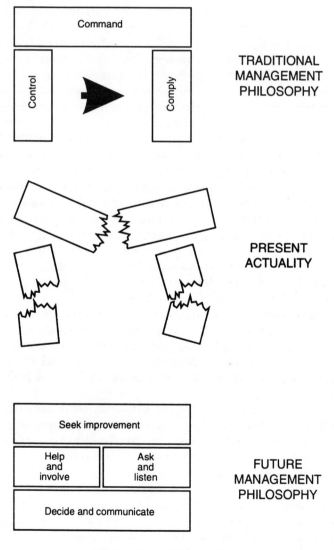

Figure 22. Behavioural change

it is still only the application of common sense, as Figure 22 demonstrates.

For a long time the traditional management philosophy of control through command and compliance provided a secure stratified structure which appeared to work. For more than fifty years it survived almost unchallenged and so permeated management thinking. In truth the five revolutions discussed in Chapter 16 were gnawing away all the time, though almost unnoticed. Then Japan, a small nation once the epitome of the control, command and compliance culture, recognised that a change was needed. Their understanding did not come overnight. The circumstance of catastrophic military defeat destroyed their secure structure. They thought long and hard about rebuilding a new structure. They carefully studied and analysed their conquerors but were surprised to find them wanting. They set about designing a new structure which took account of all the changes that were about.

It has taken almost thirty years for the West to realise that the massive competitive challenge launched from Japan was based on a new management philosophy. At first Western management believed that the Japanese culture developed a more compliant workforce than Westerners were able to command and control. In their view the orientals did not have to contend with the insidious cancer of socialism and trade unionism which were inhibiting the inherent right of management to command. Western management was so introverted and committed to their traditional ways that they could not recognise that they were dealing with only the symptoms of change – not the root causes. Western management are finally beginning to understand that education and the changing aspirations of people allied to the technological need for skilled people have destroyed compliance for ever. When the employee cannot be commanded with automatic compliance the pillars have gone and the whole control structure collapses. As in Figure 22, that is the *present* actuality.

In architectural theory the trabeated structure was the earliest answer to spanning space. In management theory it was used to span the perceived space between the thinker and the doer. If we accept the concept that both management and worker can think there is no space to span. Without having to span space we can return to architecture and that incredibly strong structure, the bonded brick or stone wall. The *future* management philosophy must be based on a bonding between management and workers.

It is important to understand that this management philosophy is designed to ensure better decisions and collaboration in implementing decisions. It is not designed to remove the responsibility for policy or decision-making from management. That is still the role of management and common sense dictates that it must be the basis of any organisation. This issue divides the author from many of the arguments about consensus, employee ownership and other forms of participatory management, which often tend to ignore the complexities of human nature. It is the old philosophical argument between Plato and Aristotle and even between Socialism and Conservatism – the difference between the imposition of academic utopian theory (however well intentioned) and the implementation of less radical but sounder evolving theory based on the realities of human behaviour.

An article by Alan Purkiss in the November 1991 issue of *The Director* magazine headed 'The death of the democratic dream?' helps to make the point. It describes what happened to Baxi, a company in Britain making domestic heating appliances, when ownership was handed over to the employees. Philip Baxendale, one of the family owners, had a grand vision of harmonious employee ownership. In 1983 the family, in an act of extraordinary idealism, gave their company to an employees' trust and the company became the Baxi Partnership. The hand-over, which was not discussed beforehand with the workforce, was widely misunderstood. The unions regarded employee ownership as a management ploy. Some 'partners' complained of a let-down by the old family firm. After five years of employee ownership, industrial relations were worsening and wildcat strikes erupted. A new chief executive, David Dry, reacted to business and market recession and made employees redundant but he also implemented a real participative culture based on continuous improvement. The turn-around has been amazing. The team-working and self-management reforms carried through by management have done more to foster involvement and creativity in the business than employee ownership by itself ever did. 'When I started here,' one employee said, 'I was asked, did I believe in partnership?' He replied, 'I haven't come here for the religion.' Enlightened management is more important to most employees than ownership. Philosophical or political prejudices apart, the essential issue is about managing an organisation rather than ownership or worker participation on the board.

The first element in the new philosophy is that management need to *seek* rather than to *order* improvement if they are successfully to support the process of change. That sounds logical but it demands from the outset a bigger change in management behaviour than might immediately be obvious. Too often management rely on the old methods to implement the new methods.

A policy decision to change to a culture based on TCI is fine and is a proper role for executives. Unfortunately the traditional way of doing things leads management also to define exactly *how* the policy is to be implemented without recourse to or involvement with those charged with implementation. Traditionally they then agonise over the best way to communicate these detailed implementation decisions to the workforce. They are now up against some of the major barriers to communication. A common language has not been established and both parties to the communication have different terms of reference. There is no identity of interest or ownership of the need to change. Management have now created a situation which makes their policy decision immeasurably more difficult to implement. Metaphorically they have started by 'shooting themselves in the foot'. Management are now limping and change may never happen.

Seeking improvement means asking for and *listening to* the views of those who will be most heavily involved in implementing improvement throughout the organisation. Listening rather than telling is the greatest change in management behaviour required by organisations who want to release the potential of their employees. Once managers have listened to the views and interpretations of those involved they are better placed to make the right implementation decisions. They are also likely to have established or at least understood where the identity of interest lies and are thus better placed to remove the barriers to communication. It is a mistake to believe that every employee (or even a majority of employees) wants to make decisions. But to understand from that axiom that employees are just not interested is an even bigger mistake. An employee whose opinion has been honestly sought and listened to is much more likely to respond positively to a decision. If the reasons for the decision are clearly explained and communicated the individuals will most often respond enthusiastically, even if the decision runs counter to their own opinion. They have self-esteem because they have been recognised and treated with respect.

Adopting this new behaviour will take time and managers will have to work at it, but it will succeed. People are 'boss watchers'. They will know from the actions and words of their supervisors that they are changing. The response is often dramatic and will in itself accelerate the change. After all, managers are also people who will respond to being treated with a new respect from their subordinates.

There is another keystone that has to be put into place to achieve the strong bonded structure of the future world-class organisation. Management must learn to help people to ensure that they are fully involved in the implementation of improvement. This has been called 'empowerment' of the people. In reality it is the empowerment of supervisors and first-line managers. It means giving super-visors the resources, time and support to become leaders rather than supervisors. Indeed, the whole process is about leadership rather than control or supervision. Allow them to challenge the way things are done and then provide them with the resource to realise their suggestions. Recognise their achievement and share their success. Build their self-esteem and ask for their help in solving problems. Encourage the new leaders to work closely with their people and a new environment of teamwork will produce astonishing results.

However, once again this is an aspect of change that will take time. Change can be seen as a threat to personal security and this attitude is likely to be most rife with first-line managers. The tradi-tional culture conditioned supervisors to control and controlling. For too long they have been 'piggy in the middle' trying to satisfy the conflicting demands of senior management. Increase productivity, ship it on time but the quality must be right first time. On and off control as their resources are continually reduced with every new cost reduction programme. Is it a wonder that they distrust manage-ment and feel insecure? To leap from theory to action without some practice could be a very dangerous move in that environment. Before supervisors can be empowered or trusted to throw away the old safe rule books, they must be educated in the new ways and trained to use the new tools of communication and leadership.

Supporting the process is therefore about communication in the workplace and empowering the workforce. It is about providing a system that allows and empowers the organisation to eliminate the 'insignificant many' problems that so bedevil modern business. Only when that has been achieved do executives have the right to concen-trate exclusively on the 'significant few'. But actions will speak louder than words. A powerful way to start supporting the process is for the executives to act on a few insignificant problems for them but very significant issues for the workforce. Principal amongst these is the working environment for the average employee.

From the analogies used in this chapter it will be no surprise to the reader that the author began his career in architecture. Young students, not yet tainted by financial priorities, are generally ideal-ists or purists. This young student (though now thoroughly tainted) never fully recovered from his discovery of the concept of the façade – in other words, the beautifully designed front elevation so often complemented by an excruciating rear elevation: what the eye doesn't see, etc.! But that isn't true; a vast number of eyes do see the ghastly rear elevation from their hotel bedroom or their back office. Similarly in the organisation (and particularly in service organisa-tions) the front office is superb but in the back office, where the insignificant many actually work, the conditions are abysmal. The daily repeated message is that in the overall scheme of things the workers do not count.

Marks and Spencer are renowned for their attitude to employees and their close working collaboration with their chosen suppliers. One of their smaller suppliers was being evaluated as a potential major supplier with all that entailed for the company in question. In general the evaluation of the company was favourable, with the exception of the standard of employee lavatories. This was an indication to M & S of how the company viewed the importance of its workers. The directors of the company were informed that they would not be considered as suppliers until this situation was rectified. They considered this an unwarrantable intrusion into how they managed their business. The company never became suppliers to M & S and are now out of business. This may appear an extreme or idiosyncratic basis for such a decision but, on the contrary, it goes to the heart of the matter. The author has never forgotten his experience in teaching quality management to senior managers in the plant of a major car manufacturer in Britain. The nearest lavatories to the training centre were those provided for the car workers. They were indescribable cesspits, but they were an indication of how management really valued their workers. Following that first visit he returned to the classroom realising that he was facing a greater task than he had ever envisaged.

Another example, one that does not reflect to the credit of the author. It concerns the computer data input operation of a very large insurance company in the UK. The task of the operators in this large room was to input all the data from insurance and assurance application forms to the company computer for subsequent processing into policies. As might be expected, the operators were measured and to a large extent paid on the basis of thousands of key strokes per hour. The author considered it a non-thinking job and subconsciously (probably in common with a lot of other managers) classified the operators who were prepared to endure this kind of work as non-thinking themselves. Nothing was further from the truth: it took that insurance company's TQM process to demonstrate the fallacy of this thinking.

In fact it was the system, not the person, that was non-thinking, but this was not wholly apparent until the process was analysed and then changed. The automatic verification of input was removed, operators were paid differently and they were empowered to question the validity of the data they were previously driven to input without question. Of course the operators knew that they had been feeding in mistakes but if they ever questioned the purpose of the exercise they were admonished to get on with their work; they were being treated as unthinking morons. The change was amazing and in fact had a profound impact on management commitment to the whole process. They queried errors at source, and this encouraged the salesmen (after the initial shock) to be more accurate in completing the forms. Double input or verification was eliminated, productivity was nearly doubled and accuracy vastly improved. And the 'moronic' operators? The lights had been turned on and they were being treated with respect. They had become the most enthusiastic champions of quality and infected all around them.

It was a humbling but exciting lesson for the author. He had denied his own ideals but in truth they had been proved right. In discussions with these individuals (not just 'operators') he found that their personal lives were filled with examples of their potential. Perhaps more the exception than the rule, one was only doing this boring repetitive task as her contribution to raising the money for the family ambition to sail a boat to South America. How easily we misjudge people by the façade of their jobs?

So in summary, to support the process management need to improve communication and help the employees or empower them to improve all their work process. They must recognise that their 'major resource' are individuals who will respond if they are treated with dignity and respect. They can demonstrate that recognition by ensuring that the environment in which they are asking the people to work is one that they themselves would find conducive to work. It may not seem much but it is a long way from current practice in many organisations.

19. FINDING JOY IN WORK

People spend a substantial proportion of their waking lives at work. Yet all too few people really enjoy their work. For the majority work is probably tolerable but provides no sense of pride. For many work is unrelenting drudgery; a necessary evil to be endured. These workers have little to look forward to, except the merciful release signified by the clock and eventual early retirement. For some (perhaps the dedicated workaholics) work brings anxiety and fear. The gnawing cancer of fear at work creates stress, which spills over into their non-working lives. There is no escape from stress and as a result their own lives and those of their families are damaged or even destroyed. This is an incredible indictment of management practices.

As we have seen earlier, these same practices do not even have the saving grace of providing sustained business success. They are inefficient and result in wasted resources (including people) and lost opportunities. This abuse of people contributes to a major loss of potential productivity and innovation.

Work does not have to be that way. There is a better way. Work can be enriched and workers can find self-esteem. As a result drudgery can be relieved; fear and the resulting stress can be removed. Releasing the locked-up potential of thinking workers in partnership with listening managers will dramatically impact business effectiveness. Above all, in the words of Dr Deming, both workers and managers will find 'joy in work'.

Senior management tend to view their operations in terms of financial parameters. There is some truth in the old joke that executives understand only three things: making money, not losing money, and money! They may talk about people being their greatest asset but in reality they consider them as an operational expense. But in their own language, they would be wiser to see employees as a fixed asset – that is, as an asset which has an acquisition and a development cost that can be amortised over the working life of an employee.

In earlier chapters we examined the conflicts caused in the workplace by the structure of organisations: the conflicting objectives of 'fortress management' and the prevailing 'expense' attitude to employees also create attitudinal conflict. Managers tend to view workers en masse as greedy and lazy with no interest in their work. Employees in retaliation see managers as incompetent, uncaring and unnecessary. In this atmosphere a host of other conflicts will flourish and pollute the organisation. The workplace becomes a battleground between male and female, between young and old, between salaried and hourly paid, between unionised and non-unionised and between many other localised groups. It is all such a terrible waste of human energy.

Clearly, peace has to come to the organisational battlefield. Not the sullen peace of a temporary armistice brought about by the fear of recession, but a lasting peace which will release the latent potential which exists in every organisation. How is this peace to be achieved? By eliminating the root causes of disharmony. When examining the nature of work in earlier chapters it was noted that the root causes of most business problems could be categorised under the headings of communication, management and people. To resolve this problem for ever it is necessary to change the traditional communication culture, change the behaviour of management and change the attitude or motivation of employees.

Communication

Modern executives are keenly aware of the importance of communication. Over recent years they have established internal communication departments or appointed individuals to concentrate on this aspect of management. Team briefings, in-house magazines, noticeboards and videos featuring the chief executive and his message are now commonplace. Unfortunately, all this communication is rarely about real work situations and is usually misdirected.

Communication is usually directed downwards from the top or some intermediate stage. It does have the laudable objective of keeping the 'people informed'. But very few communication systems provide the opportunity for the people to keep the 'managers informed'. Yet as demonstrated earlier, the people doing the job are more likely to know about work problems than the managers. But talking about 'making boxes' is not on the agenda.

Personnel or human resource departments and company communication specialists are not ignorant of the importance of feedback. They understand the concept of two-way communication and are trying to communicate with rather than at people. There is a real intention to listen and even to act upon what is heard. For the same reason they conduct or commission periodic surveys to ascertain employee opinions. They then spend anxious hours analysing the answers and hoping to detect 'positive moves in employee morale'. The comparative failure in communication systems does not therefore stem from intent or lack of effort.

The fault lies in another aspect of communication theory. The parties to the communication have different terms of reference; in the specialist's jargon, there is no 'identity'. Each has a different perception of their role and a different perspective of the outcome. Long experience of traditional management practices results in a situation in which there is no common language and no common agenda. The well-meaning communication specialists are powerless to do much about this state of affairs. The traditional communication culture can only be changed by changing the traditional behaviour of management. That is what TQM is all about.

Changing management behaviour

Many aspects of management behaviour that require change have already been discussed in this book; there is little point in repeating the arguments here. The key changes required can be summarised as:

- Concentrate on measuring processes rather than people.
- Eliminate divisive objectives.
- Remove the barriers to communication.
- Recognise that people *want* to do a good job.
- Help people to do a good job.
- Empower people to act.
- Lead rather than command.
- Listen rather than just talk.
- Retain a constant purpose or vision.
- Be a human being; not a totem pole.
- *Enjoy work* and others will enjoy working with you.

However, there is another aspect of management behaviour that has not been discussed previously, yet is very pertinent to this chapter. The role of the manager is to help the people achieve the task. The very best managers will also recognise that *they* need help from the people.

Nobody is born a manager. Some are born with obvious qualities that will help them manage; most have to learn how to manage.

Some will work hard to achieve the opportunity to manage; others will have management thrust upon them. None of this really matters; it is only the overture. The essential element is *to believe* that you are now a manager. This belief provides an inner confidence that pays little heed to the obvious trappings of management (do not deny them – they can be fun) but view it as a development stage. This inner confidence or self-esteem can see through the initial seduction of authority or power which destroys so many aspiring managers. But in the context of this chapter, what is even more important is that the manager with inner confidence is prepared to be vulnerable – to understand that criticism or disagreement, openly expressed, from subordinates is not necessarily a sign of disrespect.

The confident manager, in the Japanese phrase, goes to *gemba* – the workplace. The Western 'quick fix' or prostitution of this concept has become 'walk about management', which too often has degener-ated into a smiling walk-around and greeting people with their first names; 'Hello Bill, I didn't realise that you were still with us.' No, going to *gemba* means actually sitting down and trying to do the job for a limited period, aiming to really understand the multitude of insignificant problems facing people in their day-to-day work. No end of managers would gain insight into their business by dedi-cating just two hours manning the 'help' or customer complaints desk. Even the most senior executive would receive some shocks if he ventured no further from his fortress than to honestly observe for an hour what his personal assistant had to endure.

Managers have to be confident. They have to realise that 'soft management' or caring management does not mean weak manage-ment. Taking time over a decision which requires other people's knowledge is not a sign of weakness but the exercise of common sense. Seeking the views of subordinates before making decisions is the sign of a strong manager. A manager who seeks other views, even strong disagreement, and then makes and explains his decision will win respect and loyalty from the team. That confidence has created the team and given every member, at whatever level, their own self-esteem; their own pride. In this team everyone counts. Achieving that level of teamwork is leadership, not mere manage-ment.

In following the argument of this chapter the sceptic may feel that the author is now cheating. He has been discussing the attributes of exceptional managers and exceptions do not always prove the rule. This is a reasonable criticism and there is no intention of hiding behind some anodyne such as the sum of the parts make up the whole. But if we observe the exceptional we may be able to define some rules. In other words, it may be possible to develop some rules or structures that will encourage the exceptional behaviour of some enlightened managers to be accepted as the norm. We will return to this hypothesis towards the end of the chapter.

In the same vein, a word of warning. The author is not predicating a stream of managers (or subordinates) acting in exactly the same manner for the greater good of the organisation. That would be anathema to the concept of the thinking and innovative organisation. Quite apart from theory, it would run counter to the experience of people at work. In his lifetime he has been influenced by, worked with or been subordinate to nine quite exceptional people by any measure and been involved with others close to that level. All were distinctly different but all added to the excitement of life and working.

The author remembers two managers of contrasting styles. Both had the ability to 'inner' motivate him to achieve performances that would not otherwise have been met. The first manager was a tiger. The greatest salesman the author has ever met. His very presence could motivate managers and employees alike to commit to objectives that all thought impossible but somehow achieved. A wartime refugee from Holland with a distinguished career in the RAF, he used his Dutch-accented English to maximum advantage when it suited him. Every problem was a 'shallenge', not an obstacle. The author, not devoid of his own ego, sometimes found it a love-hate experience which nevertheless ended in an enduring admiration for an unique individual.

The second manager was an altogether different type of man. On the surface quiet and measured but with an inner self-confidence which he did not need to impose on others. He rose to be Chairman. With him each major decision about business issues or people was carefully pondered and then determinedly executed. He regularly sought his subordinates' views, usually in a request for a short paper on the matter at hand. Just when the subordinate felt that he must have forgotten all about the subject there would come a call to join him. The decision was about to be made and the subordinate was about to be convinced that it was the right decision. A sheet of paper with carefully balanced advantages and disadvantages was the usual medium. However, he could be immediately decisive when needed. The abiding memory is of a man of great warmth and unfailing even-handed courtesy to everyone at whatever level or relationship. He somehow gave all the feeling that he was interested in them and their ideas. He was not charismatic in any degree, unlike the tiger, but he inspired a deep respect and loyalty.

So what can be learnt from these experiences? Is there a common thread which is pertinent to the arguments advanced in this chapter?

Yes, there is, but it is not immediately obvious. Each clearly had the ability to motivate people to achieve what they might not otherwise have achieved. Yet each motivated in a distinctly different way. As Frederick Herzberg pointed out in his brilliant *Harvard Business Review* paper of February 1968, motivation is a difficult subject open to much misinterpretation. Much of what is called motivation in business is the alternate application of the stick and the carrot; punishment or incentive. This push-me, pull-me approach to management may lead individuals to *move* but it does not motivate them.

Herzberg argued that real motivation is to give individuals a personal generator of their own; they act because they *want* to act. That is the common thread exhibited by the examples quoted. Each of them in their different ways involved the author to the extent that his own self-esteem was somehow enhanced. The author wanted to succeed for his own sake but perhaps more importantly also for the sake of the manager in question and the organisation as a whole. His potential was being released.

Herzberg raised the question at the beginning of his paper: 'How do I get the employee to do what I want?' Perhaps in the new management culture the question should be rephrased: 'How do I get the employee to do what is needed or even what my customer wants?' The answer is to give them a self-generator. But first the organisation must drive out fear.

Driving out fear

Fear is the insidious cancer which prevents organisations operating to their maximum effectiveness over the long haul. It is created by the traditional behaviour of management. Some managers will argue that it is a powerful motivator to achieving specific and usually difficult tasks. As we have just seen, fear may move people to achieve tasks but it does not motivate them. It also shares with incentives the law of diminishing returns. Increasing levels of fear or incentive have to be applied to achieve the same movement. But most managers just do not recognise that fear is present. They would be horrified to believe that any of their own actions have contributed to a sense of fear amongst their subordinates.

It is time to be more specific when reference is made to fear in the organisation. If it is not recognised it is unlikely to be driven out. Dr Deming's eighth point in his fourteen points for management is 'drive out fear'. He states: 'It is necessary, for better quality and productivity, that people feel secure... secure means without fear, not afraid to express ideas, not afraid to ask questions, not afraid to ask for further instructions, not afraid to report equipment out of order, nor material that is unsuited to the purpose, poor light or other working conditions that impair quality and production.'

When a manager uses a phrase like 'Don't bother me with your problems, get on with your work', then fear is stalking the organisation.

Fear exists in the minds of managers and people. They are prey to many kinds of fear. Theodore A. Lowe and Gerald M. McBean in an article published in the magazine *Quality Progress* in November 1989 defined six kinds of fear that prevent an organisation from achieving the collective capability of its people. They called them the 'monsters of fear' and they are, in a paraphrased form:

- Fear of reprisal. The fear of being disciplined or even sacked. Fear of receiving poor appraisals or being transferred to less desirable positions.
- Fear of failure. The fear of making a mistake or of making the wrong career move. Fear of taking any risk.
- Fear of providing information. Managers and workers are reluctant to volunteer information which may be used against them. They may be marked out as complainers or trouble-makers.
- Fear of knowing. Information is power and many managers fear that if they do not know what is going on they will be made to look silly.
- Fear of giving up control. This fear is particularly prevalent where organisations talk about controlling people rather than processes. Managers in this environment will select or promote people they feel secure they can control.
- Fear of change. This is also the fear of the unknown. People feel more secure with what they know. They do not want to exchange an environment which they feel they control for an unknown condition.

The last fear is the biggest impediment to the introduction of TQM. These people and managers need help to recognise the need to change and a clear picture of the results.

Preceding chapters have described many of the actions required to motivate people, drive out fear and provide a clear purpose for the organisation. However, there are some further structural approaches and systems that will support the involvement of the people; that will help make it happen.

The most common method used in the traditional culture is the company suggestion system. Chapter 2 provided an example of the typical result. Most systems that rely on individuals submitting suggestions through a suggestion box or by memo fail. In the worst environments the box will contain a number of suggestions about the parentage of various managers or supervisors. They fail for the same reasons quality circles and other initiatives fail. Very little happens and there is little or no feedback. Management are not really interested and the people are not involved.

The author well remembers a planning workshop with the executives of a financial services company when this issue was discussed. The executives explained that they did have a suggestion system but it was not really effective. When asked why, it turned out the chairman of the evaluation committee was present. He replied, 'Well John, the suggestions do not amount to much; they are generally just about making their work easier.' The author's sympathetic rejoinder was: 'Yes I see, we wouldn't really want that to happen would we!' There was a pregnant pause and then an explosion of laughter from those present, including the chairman of the evaluation committee. The penny had dropped and management was about to change its behaviour.

In the UK there is a successful company called IML Employee Involvement Ltd. Their expertise is in what motivates people and particularly junior employees. They have developed a series of packages known as QED, Make A Difference and others which use humour and a campaign to encourage suggestions from the workplace. They are very good at what they do and generally a very large number of suggestions result. But Nick Thornely, their managing director, laments that in too many cases the enthusiasm generated is wasted by the very executives who called them in. There are almost too many suggestions and too few are implemented. Many of the suggestions are points that the workers have been putting to their supervisors in the past and they have used the campaign to put them forward again. This should have been a lesson or warning to managers but too often it is considered a negative response: 'We have heard all that before.'

Nick Thornely has contrasted this response to those clients who have a TQM environment or where they have developed a custom-made campaign as an element in a TQM process. The results are equally dramatic but now management respond, provide feedback and implement a substantial proportion of the ideas generated. But the key difference is that the suggestions continue to flow.

Motivate the workers as you will, but in the final analysis it all depends on the reaction of the managers. Management behaviour is at the root of all attempts to involve the people. In the author's view, once this behaviour has begun to change, the approach of IML

Employee Involvement Ltd can provide a powerful 'kick start' to involvement programmes.

The process of education described in Chapter 17 provides the first opportunity to involve people in a systematic way. Leadership education for managers and supervisors provides the comprehension of what is happening and defines specific actions to assist the cultural change. In other words, it helps to develop managers so that they want to seek ideas and will therefore both listen and respond. These managers gain experience and competence in systematic ways of analysing processes, solving problems, seeking new solutions and recognising people for their contributions. This competence is gained from practical exercises and their own involvement in task or process groups formed to analyse and define improvement goals for key processes.

The work-group education led by the supervisors of natural work groups leads to the first stage of real involvement. Initially these hour-long weekly meetings are used to encourage ownership of a need to change and then provide competence in understanding simple processes, using measurement and problem-solving. They tend to bond groups in effective teamwork. But the most important element of this process is that these meetings continue after the education and training aspects are completed. They are now regular meetings of the supervisor and the team (of which they are now part) concentrating on improving their own process. They are now actively involved in a non-voluntary *improvement group*.

A diagram used by the Norwegian Professor Asbjorn Aune in an article for the *TQM Magazine* of February 1991 illustrates this process and the next stage of involvement (see Figure 23). The titles for the teams differ but the diagram effectively illustrates the process.

In the diagram A represents the 'Improvement Group' – a natural work group within a department or occasionally forming a whole department. The important point is that they are concentrating on improving one or more small-scope processes operating within the confines of the department. Of course their suppliers and customers may reside in other departments.

The second team B is a task force or 'Process Group' set up by management to analyse the operation of a major process (for example, the invoicing process). This will require measurement of discrepancies and analysis of all the subprocesses. The intention is to establish improvement goals for the process (in the example above this could be the reduction of overdue receivables). The resultant report might include the complete redesign of the process and the elimination of some subprocesses. The selection of this team will depend on necessary knowledge. It will almost certainly include the

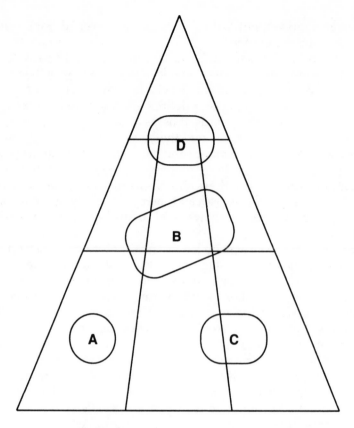

A	Improvement Groups — Natural work groups
B	Key Process Groups — Ad-hoc task groups
C	Innovation Groups — Cross-departmental voluntary groups
D	Strategic Innovation Group — Managers and executives

Figure 23. Involvement

managers of departments involved in the process and in most cases some workers actively involved in process tasks.

C and D in Figure 23 represent what the author calls 'Innovation Groups'. These are voluntary cross-departmental groups looking beyond the elimination of error and attempting to find better ways of doing things. There is no reason why these should be confined to groups of workers and supervisors. They could be mixed or operate at different levels. This is a function of the organisation and the sector in which it is engaged. Remember, the organisation could be an airline, a local authority, a firm of attorneys, a hotel or a hospital. Almost certainly these groups need to be led by specifically trained

Group Leaders. As voluntary groups they may well meet *part* outside official working time and reward could well be a factor in their involvement. The Key Process and Improvement Groups should be recognised but not rewarded. Quality should never be a negotiable issue; doing work right the first time is part of the job. Innovation can be seen as doing different work and not an automatic part of the job. It is actually asking the question 'Are we doing the right job?' rather than 'Are we doing the job right?'

The latter part of this chapter has described a systematic approach to ensuring that management and people are involved in continuous improvement. It most certainly has not exhausted the subject or described in detail all of the issues that will be met as the TQM process unfolds. But there is one important issue that does need consideration. How are we going to maintain the impetus and ensure that all this enthusiasm does not fade away? That is the subject of the next chapter.

20. CONSTANCY OF PURPOSE

Experience and research shows that many organisations have faced difficulty in maintaining the impetus of their TQM initiative after the initial euphoria has evaporated. The timing of the crisis point in the process obviously differs for every organisation. Size, locational dispersement and external factors in their sector will all affect the issue. However, for most the slide is first recognised towards the end of the second year.

Those given direct responsibility for the change process will face an uphill task if they attempt to take remedial action this late. Senior management and middle management (following their bosses' lead) have probably reverted to their traditional behaviour and switched their attention to other priorities. They are now focused on another threshold of pain. Maintaining constancy of purpose is not an after-thought, a reaction to events. It must be planned into the process from the outset.

Earlier in this book (Chapter 5 – Does it Always Work?) the reasons for disappointment with many quality initiatives were high-lighted. Many of those reasons were related to the management temptation to find easy or 'quick fix' solutions to their perceived quality problems – in other words, executives used alternatives to the TQM process and therefore those issues are not pertinent at this stage. However, three of the reasons advanced in that chapter are absolutely crucial to the ongoing success of a TQM process. They are, to highlight them again, as follows:

- Lack of management commitment.
- Lack of vision and planning.
- Lack of business measurables.

The key to constancy of purpose lies in those reasons. The same chapter also concluded that all of these disappointments can be avoided and that success lies right at the start of the journey to TCI.

Management commitment

Too many quality programmes are launched on the basis of a knee-jerk reaction by executives to a series of 'quality problems', customer dissatisfaction or competitive position in the market place. A clever consultant has helped them assess the level of waste or 'price of non-conformance'. The financial figures are shattering and quickly move the executives to action. In fairness, the consultant will have indicated some of the reasons, such as fortress management, which are readily accepted by the management team. However, very few consultants help with a 'cultural assessment' which would indicate with equal force that most of these issues stem from their behaviour and that of their appointed operational 'officers'. In other words, the executives see the results and are left to 'imagine the causes'. They therefore start committed to a policy of reducing 'the cost of quality' but have little comprehension of their part in the process.

Of course they do have a commitment to surface issues such as demonstrating their involvement. They will provide time to go to the workplace and *talk* of their commitment and some will even parade measurement charts to show that 'starting meetings on time' is important to them. They believe that this demonstrates their commitment and involvement. The real test of comprehension at this stage is how many executives immediately call for a review of all the current personnel policies: a review set up to establish which policies create anxiety or fear and could they be reframed to create trust and collaboration.

It is very difficult for the consultant at the start to develop this level of comprehension. It would take a very brave and unwise consultant to stand in front of the Board and in effect tell them that they 'have screwed up' and it is all caused by the way they have been managing the organisation. Quite apart from integrity and their future meal ticket, in most cases it just would not work. Executives are also human beings. Like the rest of us they do not immediately accept that they have been incompetent or have not recognised 'profound wisdom'. Why should they? In the most part they have been successful. The author has faced this dilemma. In his early days of promoting the quality revolution and under the spell of conversion to a guru's teaching he wanted nothing more than to seek other instantaneous conversions. Quite apart from the shallow depth of his understanding of the process at that stage he was ignoring human nature. Executives cannot be commanded to conform any more than your average worker.

So the objective of the TQM plan is to encourage growing

comprehension of TQM by executives, managers and people alike rather than instantaneous conversion. Executives, like all adults, learn by doing and this must be the basis of achieving constancy of purpose from them.

An important contribution to encouraging comprehension is to ensure that the assessment includes some analysis of the culture of the organisation. This is a very powerful tool and not particularly difficult to implement. (The method is described in the author's *Global Quality.*) When executives and senior managers see the fairly wide spread of perceptions within their own ranks as to how the organisation operates a whole new thought process is established. The evidence for change emanates from themselves rather than the outside consultant, who is merely a catalyst. It will not bring instant conversion or an immediate change of behaviour but it will almost certainly create a desire to frame a vision or sense of purpose. The results of a cultural assessment also lead to a committed pause for objective planning.

Vision and planning

This element of the TQM process was developed in some depth in Chapters 16 and 17 ('Providing the Environment' and 'Providing the Process'). From the perspective of maintaining the impetus the importance of those stages cannot be over-emphasised. They provide the purpose and the measures and actions required to maintain constancy. The plan for implementing TQM in the organisation is therefore a living document providing guidelines for every stage in the process. It must therefore be continuously reviewed by both the strategic steering committee of executives and the operational facilitators headed by the coordinator. The original plan should define specific review dates and review procedures designed to include the executives.

Measurables

The Assessment stage of the TQM process provides data which effectively establish baseline measures for the management of the process. The Planning stage uses this data to define some improvement goals and selects some priorities for action. The plan also recognises that TQM is a process in its own right and so it defines some input and output measures for the continuous measurement and improvement of the operational management of TQM.

The Assessment leads the executives to their initial commitment to provide the resources to launch the initiative. Improvement against that initial assessment will help maintain their focus and commitment. Executives are easily distracted by other issues once a decision has been made. They can also become very impatient for results. They will retain their interest and curb their impatience if they are provided with a continuous stream of relevant data that indicates progress. The key word here is relevant. They expect to see success measured in business terms. Such evidence will arouse their interest in the cultural issues which steadily develops comprehension.

The key areas therefore for maintaining constancy of purpose from the executives are the business measurables and the culture measures. Chapter 5 indicated some of the problems associated with using the overall measure of waste or cost of quality as the prime indicator of progress. To guard against this problem the plan includes some 'key business processes' (key opportunities) which contribute to a major proportion of the waste. It also sets improvement goals, many of which would be defined in intermediate terms. Measuring progress against these measurables is what is required.

Constancy of purpose within the facilitative group is maintained by the continuous measure of the process variables to ensure that it is being managed and remains in control.

In summary then the key measures for the successful management of a TQM process are as follows:

- Business measurables – progress against the business process improvement goals (for example, reduction in overdue receivables).
- TQM process measures – continuous measurement by the facilitators of the implementation (for example, to what degree is measurement being used by all as a natural part of their work?)
- Cultural measures – used to enhance comprehension of the change taking place (for example, to what degree have attitudes to communication and teamwork changed or to what degree are management perceived to have changed their behaviour?)

Auditing the process

The facilitating group should ensure that from time to time (frequency will depend on organisational factors but should be defined in the plan) an audit is conducted of all of these aspects of the process and reported to the Steering Committee. If an outside consultant was used to assist the assessment and planning phases they should be involved in the audits.

Corrective action

The purpose of all these measures and audits is to ensure that the TQM process is kept on course and to prevent wrong turnings or a general loss of direction. However, measurement for its own sake means nothing. In some cases it only leads to lukewarm approval or resignation to the fact that changing behaviour is difficult. The point of measurement is to ensure that corrective action is taken *where necessary*. Figure 24 illustrates the classic steps in corrective action.

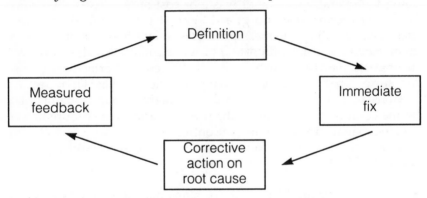

Figure 24. Keeping on course

The first step objectively defines the perceived problem. This includes defining 'the measure of solution' or how will it be clear that the problem is solved and the process is back under control. Some action may be needed immediately (second step) but the next step is crucial. Has the root cause been identified and eliminated? The final step is to continue measuring, in particular against the measure of solution.

Enthusiasm

In general this chapter has concentrated on maintaining management constancy of purpose. However, everybody is involved and it is equally important that enthusiasm is maintained or enhanced at every level.

If management is steadily changing its behaviour the people will respond. But this will not happen instantly. It is important, therefore, that the people involved should see some purpose to their own efforts from an early stage. Recognition and evidence of success are the main drivers to internal motivation for supervisors and staff alike. Success in this context will not necessarily be expressed in the same key measurables as presented to the executives. Remember that senior management are focused on the performance of overall large-scale processes. Generally the employees are involved in the small-scope processes that make up the whole. Therefore success must be presented in dimensions with which they can identify.

Facilitators should ensure that they establish from the outset some form of logging system (do not just log error!) so that the smallest improvement is noted. They all have to be published to provide the fuel for continuing the journey. Evidence that at last the 'insignificant many' are receiving attention will inspire others to join the cause. It will also show that it is possible both for the individual to contribute and the effort to be recognised. Success stories should be continuously trumpeted.

So maintaining constancy of purpose depends on the organisation keeping score. At the highest level it will also be aided by a growing customer orientation. The organisation must look outward towards its market place, its competitive position and continuously update the benchmarks for success.

Philip Crosby developed fourteen steps for the quality improvement process. The last step was 'do it over again'. In the context of this book that means repeating the assessment and planning stages every year. Nobody promised that a successful change process would be easy, but it can be immensely rewarding.

21. FROM HERE TO TCI – A ROADMAP

Organisations that have recognised the need for change tend to be impatient for action. In this mood the executives are susceptible to any passing plausible packaged solution. They know that they need outside help but at the moment of conversion they are prepared to throw away all the accumulated wisdom that made them successful in the first place. And they usually *are* successful. It is almost axiomatic that it is the better companies which first recognise the need for change. The badly managed companies never saw the iceberg and are still gathered around the band singing Rule Britannia as their own Titanic sinks beneath the waves.

This is the environment in which the confidence tricksters of this world make their fortunes. And it has to be said that there are consultants and even quality gurus who have built their revenues on answering this market demand. At the moment of decision it is all too easy to accept the logical set of management absolutes, the clearly defined methodology and the beautifully crafted educational videos, as the answer to the need. Too few are prepared to challenge the intellectual arrogance implicit in these 'packaged' solutions. In other words, they too readily accept that these consultants know the exact solution required with little or no knowledge of the organisation. The message is that their organisation is not so different that the fundamental concepts do not apply to them, but in the implementation of the concepts every organisation *is different*.

Prescribed methodologies and standard educational packages are dangerous but this does not mean that all external guidelines are to be avoided. Most organisations will need help from consultants to help them get started on the road to TCI. The specific role of the consultant is examined in Chapter 22 but the first essential contribution is to provide a sense of direction for the journey. There are two elements that can help provide this direction. The first will define stages on the journey so that objectives are clear and progress can be assessed. The second element is to agree a roadmap of actions needed to keep on route.

In *Global Quality – The New Management Culture* the author introduced the Six Stages of Quality Improvement. These have proved to be effective focal points for the planning process in a wide variety of organisations ranging from a computer manufacturer to a number of sectors in the National Health Service. With experience allied to a commitment to continuous improvement these stages have been developed into what the author now calls the Six Stages of Change.

The Six Stages of Change

Stage 1 — Awareness and Assessment

Assessment of the need for improvement, of waste, of customer satisfaction, of key issues, of organisational culture, of ability to meet change, of employee attitudes — decision to change — communicating the need to change.

Stage 2 — Organising for Change

Establishing the change management organisation — definition of vision, policy, principles and values — establishment of the quality element of the Business Plan — establishing criteria and benchmarks to measure the process and resultant implementation.

Stage 3 — Education

Educating and training all — providing competence in analysing work processes, measurement and process improvement. Focused on driving out fear, breaking down barriers and statistical thinking.

Stage 4 — Establishing Stable Processes

Management-led analysis of key work processes — establishing customer, process and supplier requirements — establishing process ownership — establishing independent reviews — implementing an organisation-wide improvement system — eliminating major problems — certification to BS 5750/ISO 9000

Stage 5 — Total Involvement of All Employees

Introduction of measurement by all work groups — establishing formal recognition — removing barriers to open communication — introduction of group set goals in work groups — introducing innovation — empowering the supervisor — eliminating negative measurement of people.

Stage 6 — Continuous Improvement

Further analytical and statistical training of facilitators, managers and key employees — widespread use of statistical methodology — planned reduction of variation in all processes — introduction of other sophisticated tools — the whole organisation involved — continuous review on improvement of the process.

The route to and through these Stages demands a series of specific actions or planning sequences that need to be addressed by management. The consultant roadmap is designed to meet this need.

A typical example of a roadmap is that used by Resource Evaluation Limited, part of the worldwide REL Consultancy Group. This company has specialised in administrative quality (as opposed to production line quality) and a substantial proportion of its clients are in the service sector. The company was formed in 1975 and was clearly a pioneer in the field. (The author must declare an interest as he is TQM consultant to the company.) This roadmap was developed from an original concept and layout designed by Faith Ralston and Dorothy Mayer of Minneapolis, USA.

The reader will note the emphasis on preparation, assessment of current position and careful planning of the process of change. The roadmap also maintains a careful balance between overall cultural change and the practical application of the principles to ensure early success in business terms.

The Six Stages of Change and the Roadmap are offered as broad guidelines to those embarking on the change route. They are of course the approach of only one consultancy and others may differ in detail. However, they do provide an indication as to what is needed and what has to happen on the journey. The reader will also have noted the high degree of personalisation involved to meet the unique characteristics of the organisation.

TCI Total continuous improvement: The REL integrated approach improvement roadmap

1. PREPARATION	2. AWARENESS	3. ASSESSMENT	4. KEY SUCCESS FACTORS
ACTIVITY	ACTIVITY	ACTIVITY	ACTIVITY
Consultant works with key executives to accomplish the following: • Understanding of company objectives for the quality initiative. • Coordination with other initiatives. • Scope of initiative. • Develop assessment materials. • Select facilitators. • Specify broad roadmap. • Plan awareness session	Consultant conducts an awareness session with executives and facilitators. This session accomplishes the following: • Senior management comprehension of process. • Opening of assessment. • Risks and responsibilities understood.	Consultant conducts interviews with executives and facilitators and focus meetings with selected groups to: • Identify service, culture issues. • Estimate level of waste. • Identify key success factors. • Determine project management matrix.	Consultant and staff carry out deeper analysis of key success factors to: • Establish measurement of key performance • Define benchmarks for improvement. • Identify and define immediate benefit potential.
OUTCOME	OUTCOME	OUTCOME	OUTCOME
An agreed roadmap and facilitators appointed.	Initial executive ownership of NEED.	Key opportunities identified.	An agreed roadmap and facilitators appointed
1 week	2 weeks		3 weeks

5. CUSTOMER VIEWS	6. IMPROVEMENT PLAN	7. EXECUTIVE COMMITTEE	8. DEVELOPMENT OF EDUCATION & TOOLS
ACTIVITY	ACTIVITY	ACTIVITY	ACTIVITY
Key service department heads/facilitators conduct internal customer surveys to: • Understand fortress barriers. • Identify department performance and customer perceptions. • Create opening of broad awareness and personal need.	Consultant transfers TCI knowledge to facilitators and assists in development of organisation's unique PLAN for implementation: • Four-day workshop. • Detailed plan 'worked up'. • Selection of tools and key education issues.	Consultant and coordinator present findings of assessment and TCI PLAN to executives: • Three-hour session. • Executives consider and authorise PLAN.	Consultant and relevant facilitators tailor educational material and TCI tools to plan requirements: • Consultant/facilitator meetings. • DTP production of material and printing.
OUTCOME	OUTCOME	OUTCOME	OUTCOME
Committed facilitators.	Complete TCI plan.	Total company commitment.	Educational material.
2 weeks	4 weeks	4 weeks	4 weeks

9. KEY PROCESS RE-ENGINEERING	10. INSTRUCTOR TRAINING	11. LEADERSHIP EDUCATION	12. WORK GROUP EDUCATION
ACTIVITY	ACTIVITY	ACTIVITY	ACTIVITY
Consultant and key staff develop and implement measurables for key success factor processes: • Understanding of process analysis. • Definition of improvement goals. • Start of implementation. • Timed to start with Activity 10 and continue	In-house instructors trained to use educational modules effectively: • One-week course with developed material given by consultant. • One-month period of practice and developing personal examples.	Theory-Practice-Action concept of adult learning for executives to supervisors providing: • Personal commitment. • Mission principles and values. • Competence in use of tools and systems. • Process leadership principles.	Supervisors lead natural work groups in understanding their work process and involving them in continuous improvement: • Personal commitment to improvement. • Competence in using measurement. • Competence in problem-solving techniques.
OUTCOME	OUTCOME	OUTCOME	OUTCOME
Immediate payback.	Experienced instructors.	Management dedicated to involving all in process.	Committed workforce.
6-9 months	1 month	10 x 2 hr weekly sessions	6 x 1.5 hr weekly sessions

13. PROCESS AUDITS	14. IMPROVEMENT GROUPS	15. INNOVATION GROUPS	16. CONTINUOUS IMPROVEMENT
ACTIVITY	**ACTIVITY**	**ACTIVITY**	**ACTIVITY**
Consultant leads audit and review of process of improvement. • Periodic — as agreed. • Measured against benchmarks and projected benefits. • Reported to executives.	Natural work groups with supervisor meet regularly to improve own work processes: • Natural follow-on of workgroup education. • Neither voluntary or financially rewarded.	Formation of voluntary interdepartmental group concentrating on innovation: • Training team leaders. • Voluntary and rewarded. • Replaces suggestion systems with teams.	Maintaining the impetus: • More sophistated statistical training and use. • Further staff development • Revisiting goals. • Continuous measurement of key success factors.
OUTCOME	**OUTCOME**	**OUTCOME**	**OUTCOME**
Process maintained on course.	Elimination of error and continually improved processes.	Released potential of workforce — new ideas.	Total partnership of management and employees.

Periodical	Forever — now the way we work

PART FOUR

Gathering up the Loose Ends

An appendix of supporting subjects

22. CAN WE GO IT ALONE?

Well yes, to some extent you can. Certainly you must take ownership of the TQM process in your own organisation. It is an evolutionary process which should take full account of the uniqueness of your own business. No consultant has a neatly packaged solution that will exactly meet the needs of your organisation.

There are two principal reasons for rejecting the 'go it alone' approach. The first is based upon internal perceptions and attitudes within the organisation and the second is based on time considerations. Let us look at each of these factors in turn.

There are many vested interests within organisations, particularly in large corporate groups, which will resist outside help. When a company is considering the internal approach to changing the way it operates, it should ask: 'How did we get here in the first place?' Internal advice is not necessarily the best. Many inside the organisation will resist outside help on the basis that the outsider does not understand the business. Generally this is true. The insider does have the advantage that he knows the corporate language and can see the political implications of each step in the improvement process. On the other hand, the insider probably does not have the knowledge or the credibility to effect change on their own.

The second principal reason for rejecting the internal approach is the time it takes. First of all, there are unlikely to be many people within the organisation who have sufficient knowledge of TQM concepts and the vision of TCI. Even fewer will have practical experience of implementing TQM. An outsider with the requisite knowledge and experience could be recruited to head the process of change as a TQM coordinator. However, by definition these are rare animals.

The organisation will have to take time and effort to gain the requisite knowledge – time in visiting other organisations, touring the world to gain experience, attending seminars and reading textbooks. The individuals selected to carry out this task have to train others, develop educational programmes and finally implement the improvement process. All of this could take years. And the company has to wait a long time before it can be certain that the individuals properly understand the process and are capable of transferring that knowledge to others in the company.

The capable TQM consultants have usually started by implementing the process in their original company. They have spent years studying the concepts and implementing the process in many organisations around the world. They have experience of what works and what does not. Perhaps most important of all, they have been working with a team of consultants with disparate skills – consultants with a knowledge of communications and education and a host of other specialisations all of whom have been sharing their experiences. Between them they have had the dedicated time and perspective to separate the sheep from the goats. In summary, the good external consultant can bring:

- Independent judgement.
- No individual bias towards elements of the organisation.
- Ability to cross the hidden barriers in communication.
- Freedom from company prejudices or enthusiasms.
- Absence of real or perceived self-interest.
- Knowledge and experience.

But before making your decision and moving on to how to select a consultant, the following questions should be answered:

- How much do you really know about the concepts of TQM and TCI?
- How much knowledge exists in your organisation about the tools, systems and techniques used in the TQM process?
- How long will it take to gain this knowledge?
- How secure do you feel that your own people will find the right answers for your organisation?
- How many times can you try to find the right answer?

If you truthfully feel secure that all these questions can be answered positively then go it alone. The glory will be yours but....

How to select a consultant

Selecting a TQM consultant is an executive decision. Embarking on the TQM journey is a strategic decision which is then the responsibility of executives. It will also need their ongoing commitment. It cannot be delegated to the personnel, training or existing quality functions. Contending consultants should therefore be invited to present their approach to the executives before a final decision is taken.

There are many consultancies and they have various approaches to TQM. Some specialise in quality management and several of the large generalist consultancies are active in this area. The smaller company may find that their trade or professional associations are capable of advising them. Some universities and further education colleges are able to help with awareness or educational programmes. A large organisation may use more than one consultancy as they progress and identify different kinds of specialist assistance they need. In this situation one consultancy may be selected to assist with the overall cultural change and another to install sophisticated statistical tools.

The contrasting approaches taken by consultancies in assisting organisations with quality improvement are in themselves a selection issue. The two most common approaches can be categorised as the packaged solution and the task force approach. Both approaches generally provide value for money, in the sense that things do improve and the money saved from the solution of problems generally well exceeds the fees.

The packaged solution is usually based on the works of one of the quality gurus. This approach does recognise that changing behaviour and attitudes requires education and a level of evangelical conversion. But the approach is heavily reliant on standard videos and workbooks and generally does not take sufficient account of the cultural issues within the organisation. International consultancies are particularly prone to ignoring cultural differences. A common understanding is difficult to achieve if those communicating have totally different terms of reference. This problem is most noticeable in videos and other educational media. The most glaring examples are perpetrated when the developers of these media, wrapped in their own national myopia, simply do not recognise a cultural issue.

The task force approach is more prosaic but does provide an immediate payback and a receptive feeling. More often this approach is aimed at specific symptoms or problems rather than the whole style and attitude to managing the organisation. Its drawback is that it rarely allows the client to take control of the process and make it his own. When the consultant departs there has been very little lasting cultural change; the process of continuous improvement has not 'got into the woodwork' of the organisation. This approach is more often provided by the generalist management consultancies.

Some consultants can make the implementation of TQM appear very easy indeed. Without wishing to deter the eager executive, he should be aware that changing management style or the attitudes of employees is not an easy or quick process.

So what should you expect from a TQM consultant? In a sense the best from both the common approaches, but with a synergy involving both the client and the consultant. This ensures that all education, systems development and communication takes full account of the cultural and organisational uniqueness of the client. Working with a consultant in changing the culture of the organisation is not the same as working with a technical specialist. It should be an ongoing partnership of interest in your success.

The key decision criteria in selecting your consultant and establishing that partnership can be summarised as:

• The degree to which the consultant is prepared to transfer his knowledge to your organisation so that you can take real ownership of the process.
• The degree to which the consultant's educational material can be tailored to your needs.
• The extent to which the consultant will assist with the implementation of the process.
• The real experience of the specific individuals who will be working with your organisation.
• The consultant's track record with other clients. Insist on references and seek confidential discussion on their working relationships.

The final decision should be based on the degree to which the favoured consultancy proposal meets these criteria. However, the reputable consultancy will be wary of producing a complete proposal for the implementation of TQM without the opportunity of carrying out an Assessment of the level of waste and the organisational and cultural issues involved.

The consultancy will expect to be paid for his Assessment but whatever the final decision this will be a worthwhile investment. The Assessment will provide a solid basis for planning a successful TQM implementation. Issues highlighted in the Assessment (in particular the level of waste) are likely to reinforce the ownership of the need to change amongst the executives. The Assessment will enable the consultants to prepare a detailed proposal and to advise on likely internal candidates to facilitate the process. It also provides a good opportunity to evaluate individual consultants in operation.

In summary, the following factors should be considered in choosing your consultancy:

• In-depth knowledge of TQM and the people issues involved.
• Actual implementation experience.
• Availability of generic educational material and the supporting systems and tools.
• Rapport and ability to communicate with executives and staff.
• Capable of supporting your timetable.
• Willingness to listen, understand and work to the requirements of your organisation and culture.
• Take account of achievements to date and other improvement initiatives.
• Cost

Evaluating the consultant's proposal

As we have seen, TQM is a process of change moving towards an organisational culture of total and continuous improvement. There are six stages in this process:

1. Awareness and assessment.
2. Organising for quality.
3. Education and training.
4. Establishing stable processes.
5. Involvement of all employees.
6. Continuous improvement.

The consultancy proposal is usually submitted after the first stage of Awareness and Assessment. A sensible way to evaluate this proposal is to consider the degree to which the consultant meets the requirements of each stage. Individual consultancy firms will each have their own distinctive style for their proposals which may not necessarily match the wording above but the elements noted below should be addressed. The most essential are the consultant's approach to Stage 2 (Organising for quality) and Stage 3 (Education and training).

Stage 2 – Organising for quality
The criterion at this stage is the degree to which the consultant can demonstrate his intention to collaborate with your people to prepare a plan for your ownership of the improvement process. Your company is unique in its objectives, structure and culture. TQM is

not about cloning the methodologies and organisations of gurus or the Japanese. We can learn from their concepts and experience but it should be adapted to our culture.

Some consultants exhibit a rigid methodology in the structure of committees and teams for quality improvement. In many cases this results in institutionalised quality management – a quality fortress to which improvement can be delegated and ownership of responsibility evaded.

At this stage the consultant should be transferring knowledge and experience of TQM to a nucleus of your people. They should then assist your facilitators to prepare a realistic plan that will work in your culture.

Stage 3 – Education and training

The importance of education and training in the TQM process cannot be overemphasised. The consultant's educational methods and materials should be examined in depth. Reputable TQM consultants have considerable experience of TQM and this is usually reflected in their educational materials. There is little point in re-inventing the wheel; indeed, there is a great danger that your own training department will invent a square wheel.

However, there are other dangers in this area. Adult learning is about identity with their own work processes. It is about learning by doing. Fundamentally good concepts and theories can appear remote if not related to the student's direct day-to-day experience. The problems of short-run production and the temptations of revenue leverage have led many consultants to rely on 'packaged' educational methods and materials. These are too often reliant on standard videos and workbooks. They also have a tendency to project the guru on consultancy. These two factors can create a barrier to identity for the student and to your ownership of the process.

Modern desk-top publishing and video technology can eliminate these dangers. The consultant should be prepared to tailor or develop his generic materials to meet the needs of your culture. Your principles, values, organisation and systems should be an integral part of the educational material. Additionally, company specific examples and the use of your logos and your own executive messages will provide identity and greatly aid communication throughout the organisation.

The common theme of all TQM education is to help the students to be customer-conscious and teach them how to always meet the customers' requirements. Insist that the consultants practise what they preach. Ensure that they are prepared to develop and modify their basic materials to meet the needs of your organisation.

Stage 4 – Establishing stable processes

This is an intriguing stage for the evaluation of the consultant best suited for your organisation. It can highlight the two most common but divergent approaches of TQM consultants.

Many technique-orientated consultants will start at this stage almost to the exclusion of the preceding stages. They tend to establish project teams which concentrate on the statistical control and improvement of specific processes. This approach can be well suited to the manufacturing environment. However, it has the danger that senior management and the administrative processes are not involved. It has been described as the bite-by-bite approach to eating elephants. However, for most organisations eating elephants is not their main objective.

Other TQM consultants so concentrate on the behavioural or evangelical aspects of change that they can forget the practical objectives. Concepts and systems must be put into practice. The danger here is that a vast effort can be put into education and training; everyone accepts the concepts and is motivated, but somehow not all that much changed.

This, therefore, is the pivotal stage in which management moves from supervision to leadership: the stage at which key work processes are analysed and the improvement process really begins. Management now understand the process and are ready and equipped to involve and help all employees.

Stage 5 – Involvement of all employees

The most common mistake in company-sponsored quality initiatives is to start at this stage. It has been aptly called the 'flavour of the month' approach. Typical approaches are customer care and quality circles. There is nothing wrong with these concepts but they will not maintain their impetus without a deep change in management behaviour; they are not TQM.

When management has been educated and has started, by their actions, to remove the barriers to communication, everyone can be involved.

Evaluate the consultant's approach to ensuring that all work-groups become involved in using:

- The systems and tools of quality improvement.
- Measurement in their work processes.
- Goal setting.
- Problem-solving techniques.
- The process to communicate their problems freely.
- Innovation and suggestion systems.

When this happens you have released the potential of your people and are close to Stage 6 (Continuous Improvement).

Other considerations

The consultancy proposals should indicate their approach to answering the issues discussed in this section and should clearly detail the following:

- Method of working.
- Specific individuals to be involved.
- Clear division of responsibility between consultant and client – particularly in provision of materials.
- Clear timetable and schedule of their involvement in the process – a phased plan.
- Any extraneous issues such as copyright.
- Fees and method of payment.
- Contract conditions, including break clauses either way.
- Measures of success.
- References.

In conclusion, the client and the TQM consultant working in partnership towards clear objectives can achieve incredible success.

23. SELECTING THE TOOL KIT

Management are generally unaware of the array of tools and techniques available to help them and their people manage the organisation. They will use various forms of measurement and most will be familiar with displays like pie charts, histograms and Pareto analysis. However, most will have little knowledge of process-orientated and problem-solving tools that have been developed to support the process of continuous improvement.

The importance of communication and the role of senior management in ensuring the continuance of an environment dedicated to continuous improvement has been emphasised. A large number of the 'quality tools' are specifically designed to help 'objective' communication about work processes and the problems encountered in carrying out operations. A key element in improvement is the facilitation of objective communication between those involved in the process and those who control the resources needed for improvement; that is senior management. Therefore, management cannot just delegate the selection of the 'tool kit' to some specialists or remain ignorant of their purpose and effective use throughout the organisation. To so do will result in 'spotty' use of the tools by some enthusiasts or lead to the whole process becoming tool-bound in the hand of specialists who will merely create another fortress of jealously guarded knowledge.

The tools and techniques available are numerous. Many are simple to understand and their use can be taught very easily. Indeed, the simplest are quickly recognised as the application of common sense. Some of the tools are very complex to both understand and to learn how to use. A few fall between those two extremes. The more complex tools such as the design of experiments are only relevant to specific functions such as process and product engineering. Statistical Process Control (SPC) has relevant applications in all functions or processes in both manufacturing and service industries. But SPC is unlikely to be suited to immediate application in general clerical and administrative processes. In other words, an organisation should understand all the tools and techniques available sufficiently to select those appropriate to be included in their 'tool kit'. The selection should take account of the timing and method of introduction as well as the specific power of the individual technique. The selection and development of the systems, tools and techniques of quality improvement as well as the training in their use is an essential element of the implementation plan. Management must not allow the selection of tools to be a haphazard exercise dependent on a few enthusiasts with the specialist knowledge.

Senior and middle management therefore have a key role in selecting the tools most fitted to their operations and in ensuring their effective use throughout the organisation. To accomplish this management must:

- Know the range of tools and techniques available and understand the purpose of each.
- Achieve sufficient comprehension of the selected tools (particularly the statistical tools) to ask intelligent and relevant questions about what they are communicating.
- Be proficient in the use of many tools both to assist their own processes and to demonstrate their commitment to the improvement process. The most valuable techniques for managements are those related to the analysis of processes.
- Use the acquired knowledge to assist in the selection of the 'tool kit'.
- Ensure that the quality education and training to be used throughout the organisation includes competence in the use of the specific tools selected; this means in the form designed or developed for use *within* the organisation rather than generic courses. This training should include practice on company-specific applications.
- Ensure that 'internal consultants' receive detailed education and training in the use of the more complex tools. These individuals should be charged with recognising areas for their application. Management must recognise that this activity may be a diversion from their normal activities and must allow the resources for training and the time taken in supporting others.
- Release the resources for all training and *actioning* of the improvements identified as the result of the use of the tools.
- Ensure that the systems, tools and techniques are used effectively as 'part of the way we work around here' rather than as an occasional exercise. Continually 'go to *gemba*' or visit the workplace and question the use of the techniques and the resultant use of the data.

With the best will in the world training in tools and techniques will not automatically ensure their use in all operations. Individuals have different levels of absorption of techniques and especially of mathematical concepts. Management and supervisors are part of this comprehension and application gap as much as the people involved in the processes. A substantial part of this gap is related to confidence in what they have learnt and lack of practice in live applications. This barrier must be addressed by management by providing help and involvement. This assistance can take many forms. The Prudential Assurance Company provide hard-bound loose-leaf binders for every supervisor. These 'Tool Kits' explain step by step the use of each of the tools in relevant applications with examples of completed forms and charts. Every supervisor has the confidence that he has a comprehensive and relevant 'guide book' to the tools and techniques. The Tool Kit is also steadily updated with examples and the introduction of further tools. This approach, together with management interest, has ensured widespread and effective use of improvement techniques.

This book has already mentioned or illustrated some of the techniques used in quality improvement. These include process analysis diagrams and process flow charts as well as the concept of corrective action systems. It should also be emphasised that many of the tools included in the quality management tool kit have been long used by management in other applications. The author is sometimes amused by the way some earnest TQM consultants loftily describe the 'new tools of quality management'. He had a working knowledge of process flow mapping, critical path analysis, PERT (program evaluation and review techniques), histograms and Pareto analysis back in the sixties and was in no way unusual in his working environment. Many of those involved in the promotion of the quality revolution should exercise a little more humility in some of their claims. Thinking and educated management did not start in the seventies and modern executives and managers are not 'thoughtless idiots'; they are seeking help and advice.

This is not a textbook and this chapter is not a 'how to use' guide to all the tools and techniques used in continuous improvement. A number of such guides are included in the bibliography at the end of the book. (A very good general guide is *Total Quality and Human Resources*, by Barry Dale and Cary Cooper, published by Blackwell.) This is a brief summary of the main tools and techniques and is by no means exhaustive.

The tools are broadly designed to assist measurement or data collection and the presentation of collected data in a form that can aid understanding of the data and help its communication to those involved. The techniques are associated with analysis, planning, control and problem-solving. The combination of both tools and techniques will also help foster the broader techniques of communication, teamwork and *collaborative* goal setting discussed in this book. In the broadest sense, leadership and team management techniques are also part of the powerful armoury of continuous improvement. These techniques are an essential part of maintaining successful improvement and innovation groups.

Measurement lies at the very heart of continuous improvement. To paraphrase Lord Kelvin, 'What you cannot measure you cannot manage, and what you do not measure you are probably not managing.' But measurement is not enough for it can disguise a trap into which many TQM processes fall. Measurement has to be *used*. Teaching and encouraging everyone to use measurement everywhere only leads to an environment in which measurement charts become an alternative to wallpaper. Measurement has to be used productively to help reduce error, reduce variation, control processes and provide data for problem-solving. A key element in the use of measurement is to objectively identify errors and problems so that management attention is secured and resources are released for improvement. For this reason measurement must be presented in a way that gains attention, calls for further analysis and leads to solutions. Following that logic the tools and techniques can somewhat arbitrarily be divided under the following headings:

- Measurement and the collection of data.
- The presentation of data.
- Problem-solving techniques.
- More complex techniques.

Measurement and the collection of data

The prevailing area is the numerical measurement of people. A cultural objective of the TQM process is to encourage everyone to use measurement to help themselves and concentrate measurement on processes, not people. Allied with an understanding of processes (simple process diagrams have been illustrated previously) a very powerful tool to accomplish this cultural objective is the simple attribute measurement chart (see Figure 25). This is of particular value in the measurement of administrative processes. It is used to record error or non-conformance with either an input or an output requirement of a process. The example here is typical of the measurement charts used by individuals or a work group involved

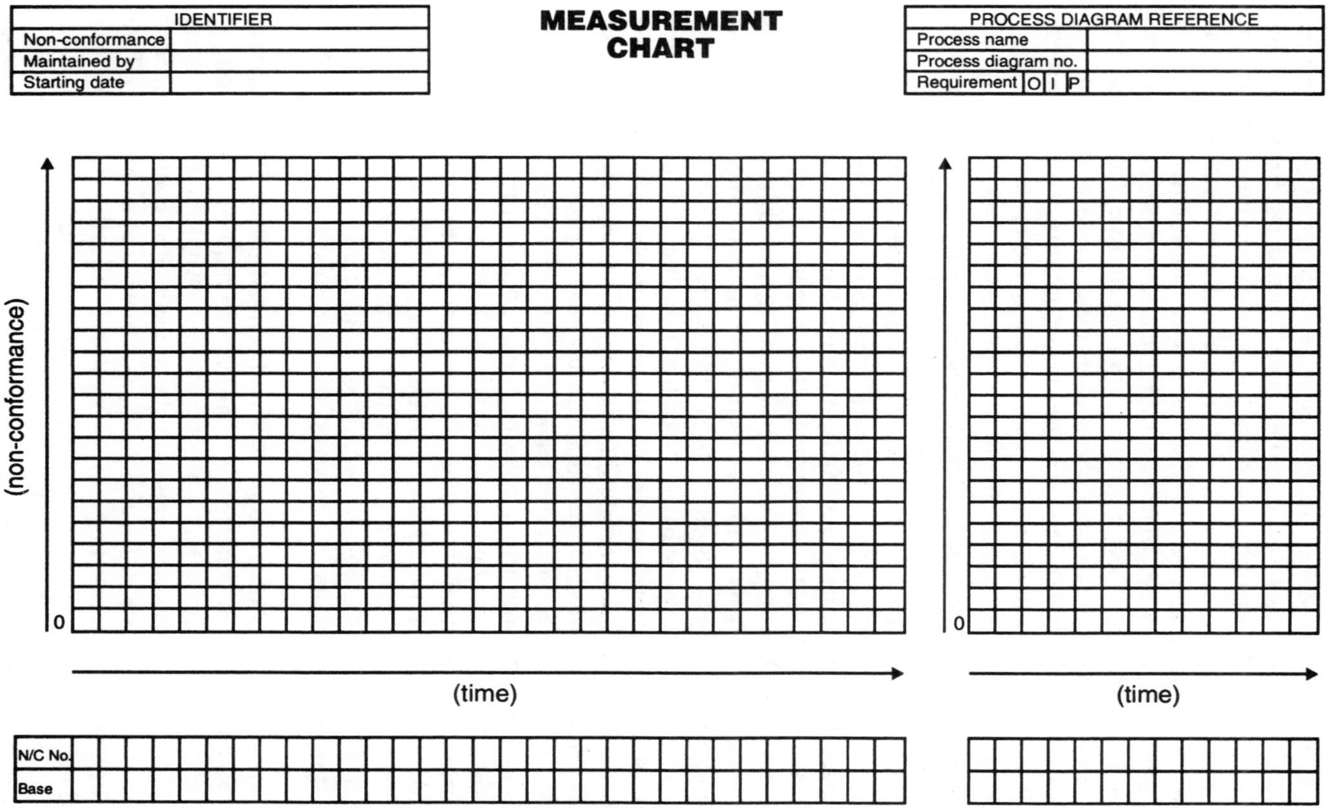

MEASUREMENT CHART

IDENTIFIER	
Non-conformance	
Maintained by	
Starting date	

PROCESS DIAGRAM REFERENCE	
Process name	
Process diagram no.	
Requirement	O I P

(non-conformance)

(time)

(time)

0

0

N/C No.	
Base	

Figure 25. Measurement chart

in a simple process. The number of errors are recorded over time intervals. The aim is to eliminate errors so zero is the base line. This particular chart could be used for days in the month and results accumulated over months in the right-hand box. The lower-level boxes are to provide a ratio with the activity rate to error. The objective is not to measure every requirement in the process but for the team to concentrate on collecting on one or two requirements, usually the requirements that the team is most concerned about. The focus provided by the measurement on meeting requirements quickly eliminates those errors under the control of those operating the process as, for example, inattention or carelessness. The inability to reach zero leads to further analysis or collaboration with management or others outside the process.

Quality costing is another form of measurement which in the widest terms could be described as putting a price value on each of the non-conformances. Quality costing is also concerned with the cost of the prevention measures used to reduce or eliminate error. The total is often called the cost of quality, i.e. failure costs plus prevention costs. This can be an useful tool to focus attention on the level of error or waste but, as previously mentioned, it is often misused. It is not a worthwhile tool for the general management of processes or the overall process of quality improvement.

Statistical process control (SPC) is a generic term for a number of measurement and charting techniques using proven statistical theory to demonstrate the *real* behaviour of work processes. SPC is one of the most important tools of continuous improvement. One could be forgiven for believing that some Deming adherents believe it is the only tool. It is widely used in the manufacturing and process industries but to date little used in the service sector or in administrative processes. It does have many applications in the service sector and is for example the only tool available in the reduction of variation which exists in every process, administrative or manufacturing.

One of the inhibitors to the more widespread use of SPC is that on the surface it seems complex and appears to require some depth of statistical knowledge. That is a fallacy and is partly the fault of some who teach SPC or write books on the subject. The concepts of SPC *are* rooted in statistical theory but it is proven theory and therefore the operator does not have to understand fully the theory or the mathematical formulae to be able to use its techniques effectively. The rules for the collection and display of SPC data are reasonably straightforward and easy-to-use PC software is available to interpret the results. Workers in administrative processes have no problem in using and understanding how computers can help them without a knowledge of cybernetics. In a similar manner the powerful techniques of SPC will in time become the normal tools of administrative workers. It would be wise from the outset for a service organisation planning to implement a TQM process to delegate a number of 'internal consultants' to become proficient in the use of SPC and to understand its applicability. They will quickly identify processes which will benefit from the use of SPC and will be able to assist those involved to master the techniques.

This is not the place to describe SPC in depth but again reference is made in the bibliography for a detailed description. It is enough here to describe the purpose of three of the key measurement and charting techniques used in SPC:

- Run Charts are used to monitor a process to see whether or not the expected average performance (within tolerances) is being maintained or is changing. They display trends within measurement points over a specified time period.
- Control Charts are used to determine whether the changes (or variation) in the process are due to 'special cause' (unique events or individual action) or 'common cause' (random variation or something wrong with the basic process or system). In principle they are run charts with statistically determined analytical data.
- Process Capability Charts are used to determine whether the process is *capable* (within natural variation) of meeting its planned performance.

In both manufacturing and service organisations many processes are designed and implemented to meet specific customer requirements which over a period they are quite incapable of meeting. This is at the root of many of the ongoing problems in management control. There is an almost automatic reaction when the process does not meet requirements that the people working the process are to blame. Usually they are not the offenders. An unaware management then provokes the whole costly divide between management and people that has permeated Western organisations. Establishing process capability is a powerful antidote to this environmental disease.

The presentation of data

Data abounds in every business and this is particularly true in organisations that are dedicated to measurement. Effective use of data will depend on how it is presented; in other words, can the parties involved in communication about work performance find an identity of interest in the message being communicated? General management experience, statistical theory and quality management practice have led to the development of a number of presentation techniques. A few are in such widespread use that they do not merit description here; these include check lists, pie charts, bar charts and performance graphs. Others, though used by many managers, are worthy of description and in some cases illustration, not so much to introduce them but to highlight their applicability to quality improvement.

Histograms are vertical bar charts used to display the distribution of data or units in a given category around a given centre point over time. This is a useful tool since repeated activities will produce results that vary over time. A histogram shows the amount of variation or distribution within a process. The three illustrations in Figure 26 show (a) that there is little variation in the results of the process in action, while (b) indicates that there is a wide variability of results. Illustration (c) shows that though the results may still fall within the predicted performance of the process they are so 'skewed' that something is wrong with the design of the process or its operation and it is likely to go out of control. *Tally Charts* used in many industries are really simple histograms, usually presented horizontally to show similar distributions.

Pareto Analysis is similar to a histogram in appearance but is used to display the characteristics of a product or service in the type of problem, error or hazard. Pareto charts are used in multiples to determine the *real* significance in establishing priorities for corrective action. Rather than distributing data around a central point as collected they rank data in each characteristic from the highest to the lowest. It is an illustration of the 80/20 rule that tends to indicate that 80 per cent of our problems come from 20 per cent of incidents or that 80 per cent of our business comes from 20 per cent of our customers. Pareto can be used to focus on issues in priority or to sort out the important causes of problems from the less important.

Figure 27 illustrates an issue which could have real applicability in the service sector. In the first chart customer complaints have been ranked in order of frequency of type of complaint and in the second chart in the order of costs to rectify the complaint. This clearly shows that the most frequent problems are not the most costly to put right. This tool is very helpful in prioritising problems in terms of their frequency, cost and other factors.

Flow charting is an analysis technique which uses descriptive data to illustrate the flow and inter-relationships in the chain of subprocesses that make up a major process. In their fullest extent they will resemble the yes/no systems diagrams used in the design

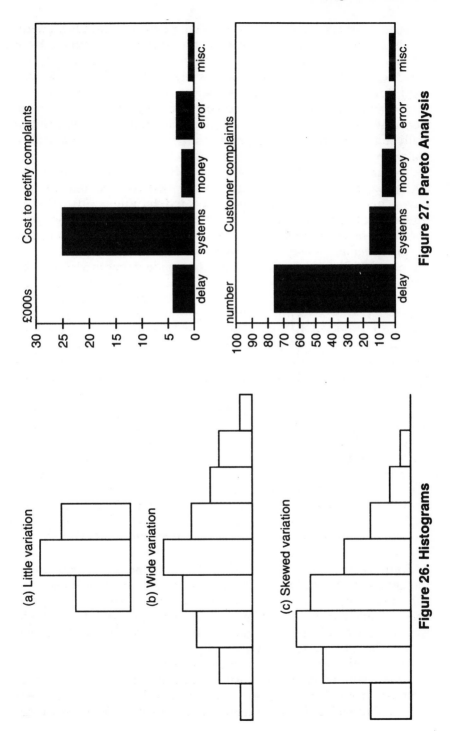

Figure 27. Pareto Analysis

Figure 26. Histograms

of computer systems. In fact they are not an invention of the quality revolution but a basic tool of work measurement and have been used for decades; such flow charts use the classic standard symbols of work measurement and computer system design. A quality-orientated flow diagram was illustrated earlier in the book to indicate the processes involved in an elective patient admission to a hospital. Generally this technique is used by a special team established to analyse and prepare recommendations for the improvement of a major process which incorporates many subprocesses running across functional departments. The simple process diagram illustrated earlier would be used to hone the detailed requirements at the lowest level. A simple derivation of flow charting can be used in problem solving in conjunction with brainstorming and 'Fishbone' analysis. This is illustrated by the work flow diagram in Figure 28. A simple sequence of events is drawn and then brainstormed to seek the possible cause of a problem. This approach has wide applicability at the work-group level.

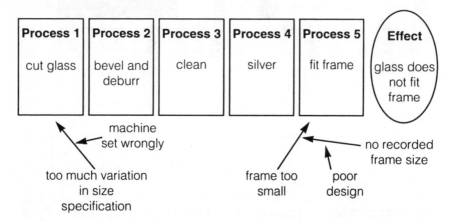

Figure 28. Diagram for manufacturing a mirror

Scatter diagrams are sometimes included in the set of tools under the generic SPC heading in the sense that they are concerned with variation. They are used to show the relationship between one variable and another. A series of measurements is plotted on a graph in which one variable is represented on the x-axis and the other on the y-axis. The aim is to show what happens to one variable when the other variable changes. As indicated by the title, the graph presents a series of scattered dots (or measurement plot points) which indicate the relationship. If the dots form a closely clustered pattern there is a relationship between the variables. The dispersion of dots or plots can indicate no relationship or a positive or negative relationship between the changes in the variables.

Problem-solving techniques

There is a wide variety of problem-solving techniques and many are taught as a standard part of management development and training irrespective of any commitment to an organised quality initiative. TQM offers the organised process to ensure that their use is more widely understood and more likely to be utilised. Most of the techniques represent a structured approach to the effective use of teamwork and brainstorming to resolve problems.

Brainstorming is a group activity designed to utilise the imagination of every member of the team so as to expand thinking to include *all* the dimensions of a problem and its possible solution. Again there are variants to the process of brainstorming, loosely entitled 'structured' and 'unstructured', which are dependent on the group facilitator. But in principle the intention is to develop as many ideas as possible in as short a time as possible. At the initial stage all ideas are recorded (usually in flip chart form) and none are allowed to be rejected, however silly they may appear at first. The results of a brainstorming session may not immediately find the obvious solution to a problem but in that instance they can become valuable inputs to a more structured process.

Systematic diagrams are often referred to as tree diagrams and are used to analyse available options to solving a problem or planning a task. The problem can be identified and the level of its importance evaluated by the available data. However, the best method to be used to resolve the problem may not be obvious. The systematic diagram provides a process of systematically searching up and down the branches to find the most effective means of solving the problem.

Matrix techniques take many forms. They are widely used in business, though not necessarily under this title. They are used to present the relationship between factors which previously might have been seen in isolation. They are therefore both presentation tools and techniques to be used in problem-solving. A variant of the matrix approach which the author has found valuable in the service sector is the *critical examination matrix*. This revolves around the five key words of all analysis, which can be used in a systematic way to help evaluate problems and develop solutions. They are:

- What?   • How?   • When?   • Where?   • Who?

These key words identify the purpose, means, sequence, place and person as factors that will feature in the solution to a problem. These factors could be further elaborated as follows:

- Purpose: What is achieved and why is there a need for it?
  What else could be achieved?
- Means: How is it achieved and why in that way?
  How else could it be achieved?
- Sequence: When is it achieved and why then?
  When else could it be achieved?
- Place: Where is it achieved?
  Where else could it be achieved?
- Person: Who achieves it and why that person?
  Who else could achieve it?

These are very thought-provoking questions to ask of any process, whether it be business, political or personal. For business purposes it can be more tightly structured into a matrix form as below. Facts rather than opinions should develop the solution.

CRITICAL EXAMINATION MATRIX CHART

Present Method	Questions	Alternatives	Selections
What is achieved?	Is it necessary? Why?	What else could be done?	What should be done?
How is it done?	Why that way?	How else could it be done?	How should it be done?
When is it done?	Why then?	When else could it be done?	When should it be done?
Where is it done?	Why there?	Where else could it be done?	Where should it be done?
Who does it?	Why that person?	Who else could do it?	Who should do it?

Cause and effect diagrams, otherwise known as 'Fishbone' or Ishikawa (the name of the Japanese originator), are the most widely used methods of systematically analysing the possible causes of an effect or problem. The diagram, which resembles the skeleton of a fish, is displayed on a large board or very large sheets of paper to facilitate group participation. In the basic 'fish' skeleton the head represents the effect or problem. Each main bone emanating from

Brainstorm each cause and write the ideas onto the diagram as shown in the example below.

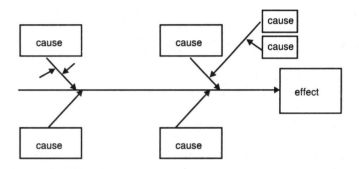

The completed Fishbone diagram looks something like this:

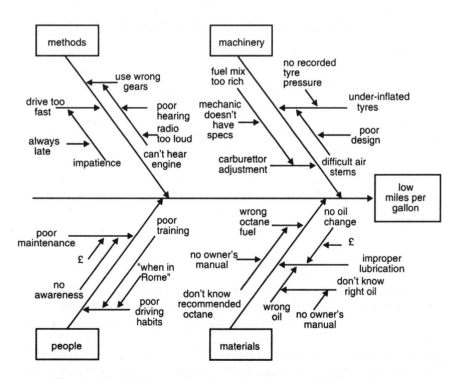

Figure 29. Ishikawa 'fishbone' cause-and-effect diagram

the spine represents a major category of cause. These could include people, methods, procedures, environment, materials and equipment. Brainstorming techniques are then used by the team to identify all possible causes which are entered on the diagram. This process often points to the obvious solution or indicates areas for further data collection and analysis. Figure 29 represents the process and is an example of a completed 'fishbone', or cause-and-effect diagram. Simple in concept, it has proved to be a powerful tool in the hands of Japanese workers and now has a wide acceptance in the West.

Nominal group technique is an element of group dynamics. Quite often one individual in a group can exert a disproportionate influence on the outcome of the group discussion. This is particularly true in the setting of priorities in, for example, what problems require to be addressed and their order for attention. The undue influence of this individual may be caused by the positional authority they wield, their ability to speak loudest or the timidness of the other members of the group. These group dynamics could result in the wrong problem being selected as the first priority and will almost certainly result in a lack of commitment from the group to work on whatever problem is selected. Nominal group technique is a systematic method to ensure that every member of a group provides input to each characteristic of the problem or issue being discussed. It is not only an useful problem-solving technique but it should also be an essential element in all supervisor and management education and training programmes.

Force field analysis is an analytical technique based on the work of Kurt Lewin. He argued that 'driving forces' move a situation toward change while 'restraining forces' prevent the change. Many quality coordinators would say that this condition mirrors their biggest problem. This technique leads a team to see and then define the opposing forces in their considered change. It encourages innovative thought to establish a balance of priorities between the driving and restraining forces.

Input/output requirements analysis is the initial technique to be used for the elimination of error. The first question to be asked when meeting a defect or a problem is: 'Which process is the source?' For every process put right dozens of errors are eliminated. The process diagram illustrated earlier (Figure 23) is a development of the old manufacturing input-output model. Every work process requires an input of material or information which is transformed by the process into an output. The process diagram systemises the definition of the inputs and the outputs and of the requirements each has to meet. In business organisations a very high proportion of error is caused by the lack of defined requirements and/or making them clear to those involved in the working process. Proper definition of all the requirements is a key prevention step.

Corrective action systems are in reality communication systems. They ensure that errors, problems or perceived barriers to improvement are logged and brought to the attention of those capable of correcting them. Sometimes this will result in the establishment of a designated task force or corrective action team to analyse the problem and propose corrective action. That team may well use the techniques discussed here. The key to the system is to see that identified problems are not just ignored and, even if not immediately tackled, remain under review. Proper use of a corrective action system will ensure that the individual or group who raised the problem are kept in the 'feedback loop' and know what is happening. This will have a positive impact on morale and encourage all freely to raise problems they are encountering. It is a fundamental step in eliminating the 'insignificant many' problems which are the cause of the majority of customer complaints. A typical corrective action system is described in the author's *Global Quality – The New Management Culture.*

More complex systems and techniques

Failure mode and effects analysis (FMEA) is an analytical technique used by engineers to ensure that potential problems have been considered and addressed. Ideally used at the early stages of design of a product or system, it can however be used at any stage and for problem-solving. The design and process is examined in detail and every possible mode of failure, including the effects and potential causes, are recorded on analysis forms. Special attention is given to those parts of a system where failure would result in customer complaints or major financial loss in failed operational systems.

Clearly FMEA has most relevance to manufacturing industry but the increasing importance of information technology in the service sector could make FMEA a useful tool in the design and proofing of computer systems.

Quality function deployment (QFD) is another manufacturing methodology which has considerable relevance to the service sector. The technique aims to identify those features of a product or service which are key to meeting the real needs and requirements of customers. This usually involves discussions with or surveys of potential customers.

QFD is both a preventative technique and a form of project management system. It is a powerful management tool to aid decision-making and to rank objectives, coordinating separate teams and the best use of technology and problem-solving techniques.

Departmental purpose analysis (DPA) is a quality management tool developed by IBM which has equal relevance to manufacturing and service organisations. It will strengthen the internal customer-supplier relationship between departments (particularly at management level), determine the effectiveness and purpose of departments and aid the development of *collaborative* objectives.

The key features of DPA (as described by Barry Dale and Cary Cooper) are that it:

- Determines, by means of departmental task analysis, what needs to be achieved by a department to meet the company objectives. In this way, a department's objectives are aligned to company objectives. It helps to ensure uniformity of opinion on both departmental and company objectives.
- Identifies in a clear manner the purpose, roles, responsibilities and total contribution of a department to adding value to an organisation's activities; non-value-adding work is highlighted.
- Describes the relationship between a department and its internal customers/suppliers.
- Provides the basis for applying and establishing performance measures by which a department can ensure that it is focusing on satisfying the needs and expectations of its internal customers. From the measurements, improvement objectives and targets can be agreed with all those concerned.
- Identifies interdepartmental problems which can be that subject of a cross-functional team.

Design of experiments (DOE) is a complex statistical technique which has little relevance to the service sector. The DOE concept was originally developed by Sir Ronald Fisher in the twenties. Over time his approach has been simplified and the most notable modern exponents of the approach are Genichi Taguchi and Dorian Shainin.

Briefly, DOE is the rational planning of experiments rather than the detailed analysis of the results of experiments. Essentially, the process is based upon identifying and controlling the important variable factors, then reducing and variation by change in design or if necessary by tighter control. It follows that tolerances on less important factors can sometimes be relaxed to provide cost savings without loss of performance.

Mistake proofing (Poka-Yoke) is the modern development by the late Shigeo Shingo of fool-proofing methods long used by Western manufacturing industries. There is one important difference in the way the technique is used today as against its old use. Traditionally the concept was applied when following a catastrophe to ensure that it was never repeated. In Japan and now more readily in the West it is being used as a normal control technique. In some areas it is replacing statistical process control techniques.

Mistake proofing is a technique used to prevent errors being converted into a defect. It concentrates on looking for the source of mistakes and then establishing preventative measures to prevent the mistake recurring. As a live control system it will set preventative barriers at various stages of the process to ensure that a non-conforming product cannot pass on to enter another part of the process.

Quality loss function (QLF) is another statistical technique developed by Genichi Taguchi. He shows that it is necessary for a company to see the cost of quality as the financial loss to society arising from measurable characteristics. The QLF assumes product conformance to the specification that is acceptable to most companies if the product is within the full tolerance of the specification rather than the target value. QLF shows that the actual loss is increased the more the product moves from the target value and that therefore performance to specification can become a barrier to improvement. By using QLF as the measure of cost, justification for improvement can be made. Manufacturing to target value reduces variation between components, improves quality and simultaneously drives down costs.

Quality policy deployment (QPD) is a long-range planning technique which has some relationship to quality function deployment. It is a powerful methodology in maintaining commitment to improvement and the other long and mid-term policies established as the overall organisation objectives. Policies are deployed down through divisions, plants or departments of the organisation. Each policy will be visually displayed with the deployed priorities for the relevant area to make its contribution to the executive policy. QPD ensures that the executives can see what is happening to accomplish the policy throughout the organisation and that every person at whatever level is clear on the details of the policy and what is required of them. QPD creates discipline and total commitment.

Quality management information system (QMIS) is a requirement for the management of the TQM change process. Information systems should be established following the planning stage to assist the coordinator, facilitators and other members of the Steering Committee and TQM teams monitor the day-to-day progress of the TQM process against the plan objectives. The system does not have to be onerous but should provide up-to-date information of progress (and variance) in the following areas:

- TQM team minutes and completion of planned actions.
- Progress of education, including details of any individual who misses modules. This element of the system could provide an automatic reminder to the individual (copied to his manager) of his re-scheduled session.
- Corrective action logs with full details of the progress of each corrective action request.
- Monitoring of customer complaints and customer feedback as the process continues.
- Survey and audit data on the use of measurement and improvement teams following education.
- Progress of key process evaluation teams.
- Details of every improvement effected, however small, with cost reductions and/or customer satisfaction and process improvements. Every area should be encouraged to log improvements for continuous publication to the whole organisation: success breeds success.

This chapter has not included every tool, technique or system used in TQM and continuous improvement. However, it should provide a broad indication of the types of techniques available. Hopefully it will encourage organisations to ensure that individuals within the organisation achieve a working knowledge of the key tools. Experience with the basic tools usually leads to further interest in the more complex techniques. The TQM process itself can also be continuously improved.

24. VARIATION IN THE SERVICE SECTOR

Executives and managers in service organisations often have great difficulty in perceiving the value of the reduction of variation. They will readily accept its importance in manufacturing because obviously materials or bought-in components can vary and machine tools will wear out at differing rates. This is another one of those 'but we are different' areas and it is a dangerous misconception. Variation is present everywhere in the service sector.

Service sector managers can use techniques to measure variation and then save money and time and improve service by controlling variation. Service variation includes person-to-person, task-to-task and time-to-time variation as well as changes in the equipment, processes and environment.

People vary; no two secretaries, clerks or managers are the same. Therefore no two will have identical performances over a long period of time. These individuals are not to be blamed for this variation for it is not only natural but may be caused by factors outside their personal control. The person with the best training, skills fitted to the task, experience and physical abilities will be most likely to complete the task without error. This individual can be the lowest-grade worker, a supervisor or senior manager.

The wrong people in the wrong jobs or untrained temporary labour create variations in performance and make errors. Slipshod interviewing, weak personnel policies, unclear requirements, bad working environment and inconsiderate supervision all cause variation in the performance of people and lead to errors. Common errors in service caused by people variation include bank tellers' mistakes, missed standing orders or automatic payments, incorrect calculations, promotion of the wrong subordinates, selection of the wrong applicants, use of the wrong form, incorrect data entry, failure to communicate relevant facts, misdirected letters and a host of others. And these errors are not confined to the workers.

Task content variation can also lead to differences in the final performance. A secretary can get a clearly written, short memo to type or a complex technical report with many unfamiliar scientific terms and hard-to-read handwriting. A data entry clerk can be given a batch of short simple records where the data on each is similar or another batch that are complex and the data varies widely. In each case, the length and complexity of the work will probably influence the error rate and the apparent productivity of the worker.

Time variations also affect quality. They are often associated with the variance in environmental conditions. The difference in performance between the beginning and the end of the day or shift are obvious. The same may be true between the beginning and the end of the week. The old joke about 'Friday cars' has parallels in the service sector. These variations are particularly noticeable in boring repetitive tasks. Similar variations will be caused by weather conditions like humidity at different times of the day.

Equipment variations in the service sector include different typewriters, word processors and their associated software, computers and computer programs, data entry keyboards and flickering terminal screens, calculators and many other items. A particular equipment variation that is rife in the service sector is the performance or time-settings of heating and ventilation systems in offices. We have all experienced the impossible environment created by the heating system that is activated to produce maximum heat on the 1st of October but makes no allowance for an Indian Summer or the opposite situation which will not accept the possibility of a cold day in May.

The point is that all the variations noted in this chapter could be reduced immediately or over time. Knowledge of variation theory is one of the most powerful tools a company can develop in its quest for quality. It can improve a manager's effectiveness and create opportunities for quality improvement.

The essential knowledge necessary has been summarised as the seven concepts of variation, which Brian L. Joiner (article in the magazine *Quality Progress*, December 1990) has defined as:

1. All variation is caused. There are specific reasons why a person's weight fluctuates every day or why sales go up or down.
2. There are four main types of causes. *Common causes* are the myriad of ever-present factors that contribute in varying degrees to relatively small, apparently random shifts in outcomes day after day, week after week, month after month. The collective effect of all common causes is often referred to as system variation because it defines the amount of variation inherent in the system.

   Special causes are factors that sporadically induce variation over and above those inherent in the system. Frequently, special cause variation appears as an extreme point or some specific, identifiable pattern in data. Special causes are often referred to as assignable causes because the variation they produce can be tracked down and assigned to an identifiable source. (In contrast, it is usually difficult, if not impossible, to link common cause variation to any particular source.)

Tampering is an additional variation caused by unnecessary adjustments made in an attempt to compensate for common cause variation. (This is an abiding sin of management.)

Structural variation is regular, systematic changes in output. Typical examples include seasonal patterns and long-term trends.

3. Distinguishing between the four types of cause is critical because the appropriate managerial actions are quite different for each. Without this distinction, management will never be able to tell real improvement from mere adjustment of the process or tampering. In practice the most difficult to grasp is the difference between special cause variation and common cause variation.

4. The strategy for special cause is simple: get timely data. Investigate immediately when the data signals that a special cause was present. Find out what was different or special about that point (for example, temporary staff). Seek to prevent *bad* causes from recurring. Seek to keep *good* special causes happening.

5. The strategy for improving a common cause system is more subtle. In a common cause situation, all the data are relevant, not just the most recent or offending figure. If you have data each month for the past two years, you will need to look at all 24 of these points.

6. When all variation in a system is due to common causes, the result is a stable system said to be in statistical control. The practical value of having a stable system is that the process output is predictable within a range or band.

If some variation is due to special causes, the system is said to be unstable since you cannot predict when the next special cause will strike and, therefore, cannot predict the range of variation.

7. How much system variation is present can be determined by performing statistical calculations on process data. These calculations set the control limits of the process. Control limits describe the range of variation that is to be expected in the process due to the aggregate effect of the common causes. Calculating these limits lets managers predict the future performance of a process with some confidence.

These seven fundamental concepts provide the framework for improving managerial effectiveness.

The statistical techniques used to control and reduce variation constitute statistical process control and every organisation should ensure that there is a working knowledge of SPC available to them.

25. STEWARDSHIP – THE WAY AHEAD

Organisations do not exist in an environmental vacuum of their own making. They are part of and to some extent subject to the social, economic and political environment of their time. Short-term historical judgements of those environments and their values are always interesting (if only because we were all part of them and partly shaped by them) but are usually wrong. Historical judgement requires a perspective which is generally gained over time. Some of the judgements of the business climate and business values of the eighties appear seriously flawed to this author.

Certainly it has been an era of great change. The beginning of the realisation of the revolution in communications, the rapid development of global competition and the rise of the concept of market-led economies (to mention just a few changes) have seen the collapse of Communism and a diminution of the centralised interventionist role of government in the conduct of business. The populist view of this era as it applies to business management is that the environment of the eighties produced a new spirit of entrepreneurship coupled with a total degradation of business ethics. The validity of both views is questionable.

This recent era did see the realisation or application of a host of innovations and inventions of earlier eras. But in comparison with the nineteenth century and the beginning of the twentieth century in Europe and America the real level of entrepreneurship in business released over the eighties is puny indeed. Too large a proportion has been short-term and in many cases has only amounted to financial manipulation of existing assets rather than the development of totally new assets. Recession is built on those shifting sands.

This may appear an overly negative assessment of the populist view of the recent business contribution to our society. However, in contrast the author believes that the easy judgement of the 'chattering classes' or the historical pundits on the ethics of business is equally wrong. There have been flagrant examples of corruption, fraud and the complete absence of ethics in the conduct of business.

As a result it has been easy to assume that greed is the only principle of modern business. In fact, almost the reverse is true of the conduct of a growing number of corporations and service organisations.

All organisations were subject to the temptations of the environment of the eighties, none of them particularly unusual in a historical perspective. The real and exciting truth is that the majority of companies refused to be seduced. We saw the real beginning of a social and economic conscience in a wide variety of organisations. Business strategy is increasingly based on ethics related to the people they employ, the customers they serve and the community in which they are a part.

It is too early to say that the modern corporation will be the leading social institution of the future and, indeed, it may not be desirable. However, it is clear that the work organisations of the future will have to put social goals on a parity with business goals. Executives and managers will have to become more conscious of the needs and aspirations of their employees, the expectations of their customers, their responsibility to country, environment and above all their stewardship of the organisation for future generations.

That nothing is new is a pervading message of this book. Most of the ideas and concepts paraded here are the exercise of common sense turned into practical application by a legion of thinking managers. So too with fundamental business ethics and the principles and values espoused by long-term successful corporations. There are of course some mavericks, that is human nature, but almost without exception the organisations that have grown and remained successful have defined and maintained very clear values. Some have been cited earlier, such as Marks and Spencer, J. Sainsbury and W. H. Smith, but in the author's experience one remains supreme as the epitome of what a modern world-class quality organisation should aspire to; namely, the world's largest professional services firm, Arthur Andersen.

The modern values of Arthur Andersen have in the main been developed from the original pronouncements of their founder as far back as 1913. These values have been continually and consistently communicated throughout the firm to the extent that they can truthfully claim that they are shared values that form the core of the firm's culture. These values provide a common focus that concentrates their people, training, methodologies, tools, business processes and policies on meeting and exceeding the expectations of their clients. The firm's culture requires each individual to take ownership for the quality of services delivered. All their training and methodologies are directed towards the empowerment of people to reinforce the 'client first' philosophy expressed in the quotation of their founder noted earlier. It is interesting that the principal goals for all categories of employees put empowerment first, followed by responsibility and innovation. These are not just time-serving aspirations. Arthur Andersen spend well in excess of $300 million annually on the development of their people and ensuring the permanence of the culture.

The values of Arthur Andersen which are continually communicated to every member of the firm are as follows:

- *Quality service:* We focus on the client in order to deliver quality service that exceeds expectations.
- *Quality people:* We recruit the best people and train them to be the best professionals in the world.
- *Meritocracy:* We provide our people with challenging opportunities for career advancement based on their effectiveness in serving the client.
- *One-firm approach:* We employ the same methodologies and share resources on a global basis to ensure that we deliver high-quality service consistently throughout the world.
- *Integrity:* We adhere to personal and professional standards that exceed those required by legal and professional codes.
- *Innovation:* We deliver unique solutions to each client's needs, providing a ground-breaking example for others to follow.
- *Stewardship:* We are committed to investing heavily in the future in order to bequeath a stronger worldwide organisation to future generations of our people.

These are all powerful values for the inculcation of a lasting culture. They are obviously designed for their own market arena but are nevertheless a model for other organisations. They no doubt have some blots on their escutcheon over time but their consistent success and reputation indicate that they really do practise their values. But one value above all seems to be the key to continued success for all organisations, and indeed, social and political institutions – that is the value of stewardship.

Stewardship is defined by Webster's dictionary as follows:

'Moral responsibility for the careful use of money, time, talents or other resources — especially with respect to the principles or needs of a community or group.'

In a period of great change and flux in moral values this would appear to be a very powerful value and reference point for any organisation or institution intending to survive the vicissitudes of change. Continuous improvement *could* be seen as a continuous state of change. This could be very unsettling to an organisation and create its own barriers to sensible development. Change without some constant reference point is not a comfortable human situation or, more prosaically, a realistic product state.

The new approach to change with *stewardship* as the constant reference point is illustrated in Figure 30. Change does have to surmount the natural barriers of resistance and inertia but it has dangers of its own to the organisation. Catalysts or evangelists can sometimes so infect an organisation that change is worshipped in its own right and then it becomes unbridled and out of control to the ultimate extent that it can lead to the destruction of the organisation. A strong commitment to a value or reference point such as steward-ship would 'hold the ship steady.'

In conclusion, the author calls for change but commends all readers to the concept of stewardship.

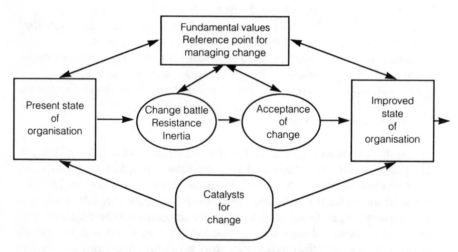

Figure 30. Stewardship

FURTHER READING

Many books have been published on the subject of quality. The following short selection includes any books which have been referenced in the text and others that the author has found helpful. This list has been organised alphabetically by author within broad interest areas.

Thought-provokers

Clutterbuck, David, and Crainer, Stuart, *The Decline and Rise of British Industry*, Mercury, 1988

Covey, Stephen R., *Principle-Centred Leadership*, Summit Books, 1990

Crosby, Philip B., *Quality is Free: The Art of Making Quality Certain*, McGraw-Hill, 1978

Deming, W. Edwards, *Out of Crisis: Quality, Productivity and Competitive Position*, Cambridge University Press, 1988

Drucker, Peter F., *The Practice of Management*, Heinemann Professional, 1989

Halberstam, David, *The Reckoning*, Bloomsbury, 1987

Juran, Joseph M., *Managing Breakthroughs*, McGraw-Hill, 1965

Naisbitt, John, *Megatrends*, Futura, 1984

Peter, Thomas J., *Thriving on Chaos: Handbook for a Management Revolution*, Macmillan, 1988

Japanese experience

Imai, Masaaki, *Kaizen: The Key to Japan's Competitive Success*, Random House, 1986

Japan Human Relation Association, *The Idea Book: Improvement Through TEI (Total Employee Involvement)*, Productivity Press, 1988

Lu, David J., *Inside Corporate Japan: The Art of Fumble-free*

Management, Productivity Press, 1987
Mizuno, Shigeru, *Managing for Quality: The Seven New Tools,* Productivity Press, 1988
Schonberger, Richard J., *Japanese Manufacturing Techniques: Nine Hidden Lessons in Simplicity,* Collier Macmillan, 1983

Implementation

Cullen, J., and Hollungum, J., *Implementing Total Quality,* Springer Verlag, 1988
Harrington, H. James, *The Improvement Process: How America's Leading Companies Improve Quality,* McGraw-Hill, 1986
Mann, Nancy R., *The Keys to Excellence,* Mercury, 1989
Schonberger, Richard J., *World-Class Manufacturing,* Collier Macmillan, 1987
Tse, K. K., *Marks & Spencer,* Pergamon Press, 1985
Whitely, Richard C., *The Customer-Driven Company,* Addison Wesley Publishing, 1991

Professional and technical

Feigenbaum, Armand V., *Total Quality Control,* McGraw-Hill, 1987
Juran, Joesph M., *On Planning for Quality,* Collier Macmillan, 1988
Wheeler, Donald J., and Chambers, David S., *Understanding Statistical Process Control,* Addison-Wesley, 1990

INDEX

The author would be delighted to receive readers' comments on any of the issues raised in this book and to share experiences. He can be reached at:

John Macdonald Associates Limited
16 Woodcote Avenue
Wallington
Surrey SM6 0QY
United Kingdom

Tel. and fax: London 081-647 0160